Israel. Land of 3 religions. The lowest dry ground on the planet. The place where Jesus was born and died. Seller of religious souvenirs by the ton. Battleground of history's most macho armies.

Simon Mayo of Radio One travelled to Israel to explore this country where almost every square inch has a story to tell. **Breakfast in the Holy Land** (written for would-be pilgrims and armchair travellers) is a guide to the experience of visiting Israel.

Simon Mayo is Radio One's **Breakfast Show** presenter. He hosts BBC television's **TV Scruples** and regularly fronts **Top of the Pops**.

Simon Jenkins is a freelance writer, editor and illustrator. His previous books include the **Bible Mapbook** and **The Bible from Scratch**.

This book is based on the Radio One programme, **Simon Mayo's Pilgrimage to the Holy Land**, presented by Simon Mayo and produced by Roger Lewis. It was voted best programme at the 1987 International Radio Festival of New York, for which it was given the Silver Bowl Grand Award.

BREAKFAST IN THE
HOLY LAND

SIMON MAYO & SIMON JENKINS

Marshall Morgan and Scott
Marshall Pickering
3 Beggarwood Lane, Basingstoke, Hants RG23 7LP, UK

First published in 1988 by Marshall Morgan
and Scott Publications Ltd
Part of the Marshall Pickerings Holdings Group
A subsidiary of the Zondervan Corporation

ISBN: 0 551 017392

Text set in Palatino 10/13pt by Jordan and Jordan, Fareham, Hampshire

Printed in Great Britain by W. S. Cowell, Ipswich.

We would like to thank El Al Israel Airlines and Superstar Holidays for their help
in the compilation of this book. Information regarding El Al flights and Superstar
holiday reservations can be obtained from their Head Office 01 439 0126.

For Hil

CONTENTS

FOREWORD

Back in the autumn of 1986, the then head of Radio 1 informed me that I was being sent to Israel with the station's newest recruit, Simon Mayo, to make a programme for Christmas.

Armed only with a hire car, a tape machine, a pocketful of shekels and a map, our journey around the Holy Land turned out to be an adventure of a lifetime.

The tranquility of fisherman on the Sea of Galilee at dusk, the silence surrounding the hilltop fortress of Masada, the emotional impact of the Wailing Wall and the grandeur of the Dome of the Rock are just some of the many images we will treasure forever.

Simon, with this book, has managed to capture in words the atmosphere of this unique land. It is an indispensable, plain-speaking introduction to any future traveller.

Roger Lewis
Head of Radio 1 Music Department

THE BORING BIT

Calling this the 'Boring Bit' is of course just a cheap ploy to make you read it. (Be honest – would you have read it if we'd called it 'The Preface'?) I was telling the truth, though, as this is the part where I thank *everyone* I can think of who has helped with this tome.

Original credits for the radio programme, *Simon Mayo's Pilgrimage to the Holy Land*, which led to this book, go to Dave Tate, who is now Head of Popular Music at the BBC World Service. Also to Johnny Beerling, Doreen Davies, Stuart Grundy and Dave Price at Radio 1 for their encouragement. The programme would not have worked without its producer, Roger Lewis, and engineer, Brian Thompson, whose combined brilliance made my ramblings a coherent 90 minutes.

And this book wouldn't have worked without the skills of Simon Jenkins, writer, cartoonist, cartographer and all-round clever dick. Cheers, mate. Also thanks to Stephen Butler for putting up with looking at my mug through a camera lens for the photographs. Thanks to Russ for his dubious driving skills and to Peter for his never-ending enthusiasm.

I'd also like to thank my wife, my parents, my brother, my sister, her husband, their children, my grandmother, my mother-in-law, her parents and everyone else who knows me.

Simon Mayo.

ARRIVING FOR BREAKFAST

If you travel to the Holy Land, you'll probably find that your journey starts at the dead of night in some corner of an airport. Travelling by El Al (Israel's national airline), everyone is treated as a potential terrorist. You're split up from the other people travelling with you, and politely grilled by at least two members of the El Al staff.

'Is this your first visit to Israel?'

'How long are you staying?'

'When did you pack your bag?'

'Could anyone have slipped something in your bag when you weren't looking?'

'When did you meet the people travelling with you?' Etc, etc.

By the time they've finished, even if you *know* you've got nothing to hide, you *feel* guilty and you're sure they'll never allow you on the plane! But the great thing is that you can travel in almost 100 per cent safety, knowing how difficult it would be to get anything dangerous onto the plane after all that. El Al must have one of the best safety records around, which counts for a lot in the age of hijacks.

More than Just a Holiday

All the obsession with security is a reminder that Israel is one of the world's hot spots. Israel is always in the news, as the Palestinian Arabs and the Israelis argue over who the land belongs to. The country is only the size of a postage stamp, and yet many of the world's major armies have gone to war over this piece of territory.

But if it's one of the most argued-about countries, it's also one of the most well-loved. Three of the world's great religions have their holy sites here: Judaism, Islam and Christianity. And for Jews especially, this land is at the heart of their faith. The Jewish people have a saying: 'Next year in Jerusalem'. They long to be in Israel, and a visit there is more than just a holiday, it's a *pilgrimage* (a journey made for religious reasons). Christians and Muslims have also been making pilgrimages to the Holy Land ever since their faiths came into existence.

For people who don't have any particular faith that they stick to, a visit to Israel can still be something of a pilgrimage. Standing in some of the places where Jesus suffered, or walking where he walked, can make you think twice about what you really *do* believe in!

Flying Out

On the plane, you see a cross-section of the people who travel out to Israel. In the back seats there's Darren and Sharon, heading for two weeks on Israel's Mediterranean beaches, their hand luggage sopping wet with burst tubes of Factor 33 sun tan lotion. Sitting over the wing is an old white-haired couple, two Polish Catholics, who've been saving up for years for this visit to Israel's holy places.

Also at the back of the plane (looking disapprovingly at Darren and Sharon) is a group of Jewish men wearing dark suits and skullcaps, with long thin strands of hair falling down onto their shoulders. In Club Class at the very front are two American businessmen discussing their business in voices loud enough to be heard by the Jewish men at the back of the plane. And by one of the windows near the galley is a young, thin Jewish boy with a haircut out of the 1950s. He's bent over a black, religious-looking book, muttering prayers under his breath and rocking backwards and forwards.

It's then that you realise that you're not travelling to an *ordinary* country!

First Taste of the Holy Land

After a few hours of flying through the darkness, the sun comes up and suddenly out of the window you can see the long, straight coast of Israel below. It's hard to describe, but a sort of thrill runs through the passengers on the plane as they see the land below for the first time. And then, a few minutes later, as the wheels hit the runway, the cabin fills with applause from the travellers.

And then, after baggage reclaim, passport-stamping and customs, there's breakfast. Breakfast in the Holy Land is pretty different from breakfast in a British Transport Caf! Some of the menu items you might be faced with are...black olives, roll-mop herring, yog-hurt and cucumber, pickled vegetables, chick-pea paste, sliced meats, flat-baked bread...Breakfast is big business in Israel.

After that, it's only an hour's journey from Ben Gurion airport up through the hills to Israel's capital city, Jerusalem. However, in this book we're going to save Jerusalem till last. Our first stop on our travel round the Holy Land will be the place where Jesus' mother, Mary, heard some news about the patter of tiny feet...

1 NAZARETH AND BETHLEHEM

This is really where the story all begins – Nazareth, the place where Jesus grew up. Two thousand years ago it was just a small, sleepy northern town. If they'd had maps in those days, then Nazareth probably wouldn't have been on them. Some people living then even saw Nazareth as a bit of a joke. The Bognor Regis of the Holy Land. It certainly wasn't the kind of place where you'd expect Messiahs to come from!

Nazareth streets. It isn't quite how you imagine the place should be. It's a modern town with the past hidden away in the depths of its churches.

Modern Nazareth

Over the 2,000 years since Jesus first learned to walk here, the place has changed. Probably for the worse. It's no longer the quiet, insignificant little place it used to be – although the guidebooks still delight in describing it as 'nestling' in a hollow in the Galilean hills. It actually sprawls over them pretty untidily.

Nazareth now boasts a population of about 40,000 – split equally between Christians and Muslims. Walking around in the streets of Nazareth (trying not to get run over!) it doesn't really seem a very holy place. With its chocolate factory, fast-food restaurants, garages and markets, it seems to be a very ordinary, commercial town. So what's so special about it?

Stranger in the Night

What put Nazareth on the map for Christians was that it was here that Mary, Jesus' mother, lived. And it was in Nazareth that she was visited one night by a messenger from God. This messenger, the Archangel Gabriel, was God's right-hand angel. Getting a visit from him was only second-best to getting a call from God himself.

Mary (who was probably around 16 or so) was naturally terrified at meeting such a being. But not only was his visit a shock, but the news he had to tell her was pretty shocking, too. Over to the Bible...

The angel said to her, 'Don't be afraid, Mary; God has been gracious to you. You will become pregnant and give birth to a son, and you will name him Jesus. He will be great and will be called the Son of the Most High God...'

Pregnant Virgin Shock Horror

It was hardly a dream come true for a young, unmarried girl in those days to be woken up in the middle of the night to be told 'you're pregnant'! Mary was about to be married to Joseph, a local carpenter. They were probably a hard-working, respectable couple. Everyone thought they were rather sweet. They were engaged and everything seemed to be going just right for them.

Then, all of a sudden, *Mary's pregnant.*

Now what is everyone in Nazareth going to think? 'Oh, it's probably the Archangel Gabriel again'? It's unlikely. There was probably a real scandal, a lot of gossip, a couple of angry families, friends who thought Mary had become a Moonie, and all the rest.

The Church of the Annunciation in Nazareth. Is this where Mary met the Angel Gabriel?

You can imagine what the *Sun* would have made of it.

On top of all that, it was pretty dangerous in those days to get pregnant before marriage. The penalty, if it was strictly carried out to the letter of the law, was death by stoning.

The amazing thing is that Mary didn't complain about the news. She knew what it would mean for her and Joseph, but her faith was so strong that she was able to accept that this was what God wanted. From the Bible again...

> *'I am the Lord's servant,' said Mary; 'may it happen to me as you have said.' And the angel left her.*

Time-Warps

Apart from the *Nazareth Fried Chicken*, there are at least two really good places to visit in Nazareth, which take you back to those events in the life of Mary.

The first is the Basilica of the Annunciation. ('Annunciation' being the 'announcement' made by Gabriel.) This church is easy to spot – it's in the centre of town, with a big cone-topped tower. The church was built by Franciscans in 1966, but it stands on the ruins of two other, much older churches.

Tradition has it that this is the place where Mary met the angel. Inside, the church is softly lit and thankfully very quiet after the noise in the streets outside. It has two storeys. Upstairs is a collection of

Unlikely that this was around for Jesus to pop into.

pictures of Mary and her child sent in from churches all over the world. Each country has shown Mary and Jesus as if they were from their country. So there's a Japanese Jesus, an African Jesus, and so on.

Downstairs is a large gallery that looks down into a cave in the rock. Many people believe this is the exact spot where Mary heard she was pregnant. And they may well be right – Christians have venerated this place for almost as long as Christianity has been around.

The second place to see is St Gabriel's Church, which is built over ancient Nazareth's only spring. The spring now runs in the crypt of the church! This is where Mary used to come to get water for her family,

In just about all of Israel's holy places, you meet signs like this. The rule seems to be that your shoulders and your thighs have to be covered up. If you don't, then you could get chucked out, or get a stone or three lobbed in your direction

17

and according to one tradition, *this* is the spot where Mary and Gabriel met. This isn't the last time that we'll meet rival sites for holy happenings in Israel.

In the end, Mary and Joseph only had to put up with the scandal for a few months. Suddenly, the Romans announced they were doing a census. Everyone had to be counted at the town they were born in. That's when Mary and Joseph put all their belongings on a donkey, saddled up and started that now rather famous trip to Bethlehem.

Road to Bethlehem

It's hard to believe that Bethlehem *really* exists. And yet as you drive on the busy road that goes south out of Jerusalem, there it is on the roadsigns. Bethlehem. And the only place you've seen it written before is on Christmas cards, with shepherds, stars, donkeys, wise men, mangers and stables all over them. So it's a bit of a shock when you see your first Bethlehem roadsign.

The next shock is when you pass the Bethlehem Tobacco and Cigarette Company! It's then that you start to realise that like Nazareth it's in some ways an ordinary town.

If you're hungry then you can always grab a bite to eat at a place called The Christmas Tree. And then there's the Holy Manger Stores, full of religious souvenirs. But sadly you *won't* find a stick of rock with 'Bethlehem' written all the way through it.

Manger Square etc

In the middle of Bethlehem is a place called Manger Square. It's full of parked cars and buses, soldiers keeping an eye on things, and streetwise kids offering to 'look after' your car while you're gone. And there's often tension in the air. In a neighbouring village, local Palestinians regularly throw stones at the Israeli troops, who they see as enemy-occupying troops. The women have even been known to take off their high heels so that they can throw stones more easily!

Coming to Manger Square is the whole reason why pilgrims come to Bethlehem, because just off the square is the Church of the Nativity – the place where it's believed Jesus was born.

The building looks more like a fortress than a church. It's actually one of the oldest churches in the world. It was started by the Roman Emperor Constantine in the year 325 – or more accurately, by his Mum, Helena. She had this thing about building churches over Israel's holy sites. More about Helena later.

You can't just walk into the church, because the doorway is so low. They obviously had problems, centuries back, with infidels riding into the church on horseback (or camels), so they fitted the place with the equivalent of speed bumps.

You actually have to bow down and stoop to enter the doorway – it's about four feet high. It's quite appropriate, because you have to humble yourself a bit before you can get in here.

Just outside the door, there's an interesting notice on the wall. It tells you how you're expected to behave inside the church. There are lots of notices like this all over Israel, but this one really says the lot. Here's a selection…

- Smoking is prohibited
- Absolute silence is urged
- Modest dress demeanour is essential
- Eating and drinking within these precincts are absolutely forbidden
- The bringing in of animals is forbidden
- Arms may not be taken within the church
- Photographs may be taken, but not of members of the clergy

It seems that there's still no shortage of smoking, drinking, gun-carrying camel-riders who want to get inside the Church of the Nativity for a shot of the clergy...

Another Church with a Cave!

The Church of the Nativity feels rather strange. From the back, just after stepping through the door, it looks quite empty and bare. This isn't all that surprising, as there are no pews, no seats, nothing! Just two rows of dark red columns, a very high roof that was once made from English oak (a present from our King Edward IV) and some very aged mosaics that you can see under trapdoors in the floor.

The lack of seats is pretty standard in many oriental churches, where you have to stand for services that can go on for over three hours. After that, even a hard pew would feel like heaven!

If you're a history nut, you'd be interested to spot the most strange item in this strange church – a picture of King Canute on the fourth column on the right, painted by the Crusaders when they were over here over 800 years ago. And the church was ancient when *they* visited it!

In contrast to the back of the church, the altar area at the front is very ornate. Underneath it is a small, natural cave, where, tradition states, Mary gave birth to Jesus. Going to the right of the altar, you pass a priest manning a modest little stall of candles, incense, and bottles of guaranteed holy water taken from the River Jordan. And then you go down a flight of marble steps under an arch into the cave known as the Grotto of the Nativity.

It really *is* a cave – except that the rock walls have been covered in some very dirty, gloomy old tapestries, heavy with the smell of centuries of incense. There's enough incense down there to turn you into a secondary smoker. At the foot of the steps, there's a small area on the left called the Chapel of the Manger. Here Mary is said to have placed Jesus after he was born. And then to your right is the place of the birth, where there is a big indentation in the rock. If it doesn't sound too irreverent, this actually looks like a very large fireplace.

You have to get down on your hands and knees to look inside. What you see there is an old, cracked marble slab with two candles burning on it. A whole collection of tinsely oil lamps hang over the top like a cluster of bats. In front of the candles, set into the marble, there is a large silver star. Written around the star in Latin are the words, 'Here Jesus Christ was born of the Virgin Mary'.

This star, set in the marble floor of the cave under Bethlehem's Church of the Nativity, is said to mark the spot where Jesus was born. People come from all over the world just to be here.

Slices of History

Israel is a land with a lot of history. It's also got great beaches, good places to eat, a fantastic climate, and the Dead Sea (where it's next-to-impossible to drown). But history is Israel's speciality.

In this book, we'll occasionally have to mention some of the different historical eras. If you get a bit lost, feel free to come back to this box for a lightning guide to a few of the different layers of history.

Old Testament

This refers to the time in Israel's history before the birth of Christ – as recorded in the first half of the Bible.

Roman

During Jesus' lifetime, Israel was just a small piece of the Roman Empire, which ruled the whole Mediterranean. The Jewish people resented the Romans (especially their troops of occupation and high levels of tax) and there were all sorts of plots around to rebel against their harsh rule.

Byzantine

After the Roman Emperor was converted to Christianity in AD 313, Jerusalem came under Roman-Christian rule. This lasted until AD 638 when the city was conquered by Muslims.

Crusader

The Crusaders were European troops who saw it as their holy duty to recapture the Holy Land from the Muslims. Their two brief periods of rule lasted just over 100 years (starting from 1099). They rebuilt the Church of the Holy Sepulchre.

Turkish

Israel became part of the Turkish (or Ottoman) Empire in 1517. Suleiman the Magnificent (who built the present-day walls of Jerusalem) was one of this empire's rulers. Turkish rule ended during World War 1, when Jerusalem surrendered to the British. They acted as caretakers of Israel until 1948.

State of Israel

Since 1948, Israel has been an independent state, the homeland of the Jewish people.

There is a fuller sketch of Israel's history at the end of the book.

Violent Vicars

All this isn't exactly everyone's cup of tea – and the place can be profoundly disappointing. It is supposed to be one of the holiest pieces of ground in the world, and yet at the busiest times of the year you can be herded in as if you're entering Santa's Grotto. The cave itself felt as packed (and about as holy) as a tube train.

What makes it worse is that various branches of the Christian church jealously guard their rights here. The Armenians, the Greek Orthodox and the Roman Catholics all have their own zones within the church. They have been known to hold long and bitter disputes over who should mop step number 6, who should stand where in processions, and where the no-go areas are. It's sad to think that you can get GBH in this church from a fellow-Christian simply for sweeping the wrong step.

All this violence makes you wonder if there's a more sinister reason for the lack of chairs in the church upstairs. Were they all destroyed in an epic chair-throwing fight between the Greeks and Armenians?

The crowning glory is that in the nineteenth century, some Christians in the church removed the silver star. This led to an argument between France and Russia that eventually escalated into the Crimean War. So the Church of the Nativity can be very disappointing. It's supposed to be the place where the prince of *peace* was born.

Did it Happen Here?

On the plus side, it seems that the cave really could be where it all happened. Many Bethlehem houses had caves in the time of Jesus. Houses were built on top of them, and the cave was used as a sort of downstairs, where the animals slept at night. From the very early days of the Christian faith, this particular cave was identified as *the* place where Jesus took his first lungful.

If you can forget the religious squabbles and see through all the marble, incense and silver trinkets, then it's amazing to think that Jesus might have been born *here*. As the Book of Luke puts it...

While Mary and Joseph were in Bethlehem, the time came for her to have her baby. She gave birth to her first son, wrapped him in strips of cloth and laid him in a manger – there was no room for them to stay in the inn.

But why all the fuss anyway about the *birth* of Jesus? Christians believe that Jesus was God coming to Earth as an ordinary human being. So this moment when it all happened – when God humbled himself to become the helpless baby of a peasant couple – is obviously very special.

Many of the people who come down those steps into the cave under Bethlehem's church aren't tourists wanting pictures for their family albums. They come as pilgrims, making the journey of a lifetime. They come to pray and worship the God who became a human being. That's why it's worth making the effort to go to Bethlehem and to try to get in touch with what happened there so long ago.

This Chapter's
Hit List...

Jericho

Dead Sea

Ein Gedi

Masada

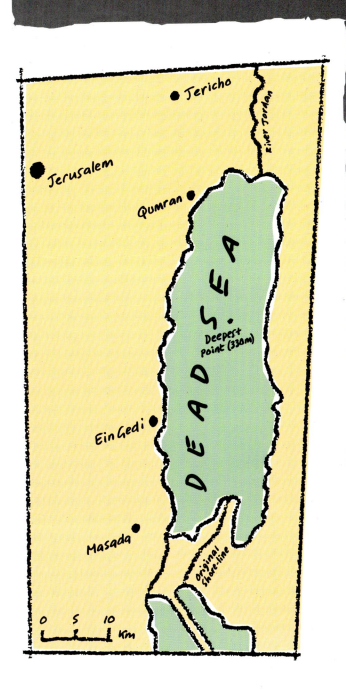

Jericho

Jerusalem

River Jordan

Qumran

DEAD SEA
Deepest
Point (330m)

Ein Gedi

Masada

Original Shore-line

0   5   10
         Km

The next scene in the story of Jesus' life takes us into the desert. Suddenly Jesus is about 30 years old. The Bible doesn't tell us a lot about Jesus between his birth in that Bethlehem cave, and his life as an adult. What we do know is that he grew up in Nazareth, and probably learnt how to be a carpenter from his Dad.

So why the desert? Because it was somewhere around here that Jesus switched over from being just another bloke who was handy with a Black & Decker and started his new life – as a preacher, healer and all-round miracle worker.

The World's Deepest Desert

This desert is called the Judean Desert, and it's just

Finding your way around in Israel can get confusing. Many places have two names – an ancient and a modern one ! For example, Nablus and Shechem are one and the same. This shelter is near Jericho, with the hills at the edge of the Jordan valley in the background.

to the east of Jerusalem. You take the road to Jericho and very quickly find yourself praying that the brakes are in good order. The road just drops and drops until you reach a large concrete pillar which announces that you are now at sea level. And from there the road just keeps on dropping.

This road is really rather famous, because it found its way into one of Jesus' parables – the Parable of the Good Samaritan. Jesus told the story of a man who travelled this road on his donkey, when he was attacked by a bunch of thieves who left him half-dead and minus his cash. Looking around at the scenery as the road goes even further below sea-level, it's easy to see it as ideal bandit territory. The land is riddled with little hills and steep ravines for the perfect quick getaway. Even a fully-armed Securicor van would feel a bit nervous doing this run.

Then suddenly the road comes out of the desert hills and onto a wide plain. This is the Jordan Valley that runs from north to south in Israel. It's a massive trench, well below sea-level, in which the River Jordan runs from the Sea of Galilee down to the Dead Sea. It's a stunning view, with the hills marching north on your left, and the top end of the Dead Sea shimmering away on your right.

On the Borderline

Across the other side of this massive valley are the hills of Jordan – Israel's neighbour to the east. The two countries have often been at war, and are still hostile to each other. The border between them runs right down the river and across the middle of the Dead Sea. As you follow the road north, alongside the river, there are formidable, twin barbed-wire fences to stop anyone from getting across. Just a gentle reminder that this beautiful country is one of the most argued-over bits of land in the world.

It can be a bit of a shock to see Israeli soldiers casually carrying machine guns on the streets. The tensions between Arabs and Jews often crackles into violence and bloodshed.

One thing that Jordan sends over that barbed-wire fence into Israel is its airwaves. You can listen to Radio Jordan while you're travelling around as it has a good mix of Western pop plus all the local news, told with an Arab bias. King Hussein, the ruler of Jordan, gets a mention in most of the bulletins, even if he hasn't done anything very exciting. And you can almost hear the announcers bowing as they say his name: 'His Majesty King Hussein stubbed his toe as he arose from bed this morning...'

Jesus and the Temptations

The River Jordan isn't a very impressive river, but it's the best that a hot country like Israel can manage. It was in this river, probably somewhere around Jericho, that Jesus was baptized and began the work that was to make him famous – and that was to have him put to death. Jesus was baptized here by a fiery, fanatical preacher called John the Baptist, whose idea of a good time was to walk around in camel's hair clothes and to eat locusts and wild honey (a bit like muesli).

After his baptism, Jesus went up into the hills. He spent forty days there without food, and he was tempted (unsuccessfully) by the Devil, who wanted him to give up his work before it had even begun. Just outside Jericho, there's a Mount of Temptation, where it was all supposed to have happened. And in Jericho itself, you can find the 'Mount of Temptation Restaurant'. Despite its name, the menu in the window *isn't* very tempting…

Walls Came Tumbling Down

Jericho, of course, is famous for other things as well. For a start, it's the oldest-known town in the world (people started building here around 10,000 years ago). But Jericho is even more famous for its walls. They collapsed when the people of Israel, led by their military leader Joshua, crossed the Jordan from the east and entered the 'Promised Land' – the land promised to them by God. In those days Jericho was a strong city, hostile to the Israelites.

In a famous scene, the Israelites were told by God not to attack the walls with weapons, but simply by marching around them…

Guess what this says!

You and your soldiers are to march around the city once a day for six days… On the seventh day you and your soldiers are to march around the city seven times while the priests blow the trumpets. Then they are to sound one note. As soon as you hear it, all the men are to give a loud shout, and the city walls will collapse.

29

Jericho has been an oasis town in the middle of the desert for more centuries than most people have had birthdays!

And according to reports, this plan worked like a dream. You can visit the site of ancient Jericho, which is just outside the modern town – but don't bother looking too hard for the walls.

Today, Jericho is a pleasant-looking oasis town, with tall palm trees bordering the road as you drive in. But even this town isn't immune from the violence that plagues Israel. A Palestinian was recently killed in Jericho by other Palestinians for being an informer.

Blinded by the Light

Jesus passed through Jericho many times. One time he encountered a blind man called Bartimaeus who used to beg for his living, just outside town. It was a couple of years after his baptism, and Jesus was on his way up to Jerusalem with his disciples...

As Jesus was coming near Jericho, there was a blind man sitting by the road, begging. When he heard the crowd passing by, he asked,'What is this?'

'Jesus of Nazareth is passing by,' they told him.

He cried out, 'Jesus! Son of David! Take pity on me!'

The people in front scolded him and told him to be quiet. But he shouted even more loudly, 'Son of David! Take pity on me!'

So Jesus stopped and ordered the blind man to be brought to him. When he came near, Jesus asked him, 'What do you want me to do for you?'

'Sir,' he answered, 'I want to see again.'

Jesus said to him. 'Then see! Your faith has made you well.'

At once he was able to see, and he followed Jesus, giving thanks to God.

The Dead Sea

In this area, there are other interesting places to see which aren't connected with the life of Jesus. You turn left to reach Jericho off the road running down from Jerusalem. But if you turn right instead, then you end up at the Dead Sea, the lowest point on Earth. And it's a sobering thought. For many visitors to the Dead Sea, this is the nearest they're ever going to get to Australia.

If you go down to the water's edge, your feet are standing on the lowest dry ground on the planet. You are 1,285 feet below the level of the Mediterranean, only fifty miles away. At its deepest, the sea goes down another 1,300 feet. Here are some more amazing facts about this unearthly place...

- The Dead Sea is fed by the River Jordan, plus innumerable hot springs. But the area is so hot that the sea loses more water in evaporation than it gets.

- Because of this, the Dead Sea is a massive chemical bath. It's thick with potassium, sodium, magnesium and a host of other nasties – five times more salty than ordinary sea water.

The Dead Sea is drying up. And as the water recedes, it leaves behind acres of salt in weird formations.

● As it evaporates, the sea is gradually shrinking – there's now dry land in the middle of it.

● It's the only sea in the world that doesn't have even a single fish. There are no nutters lining the shore here to get sight of an Israeli version of the Loch Ness Monster.

Ready Salted

If there was a real sea on the Moon, then it would look something like this. The Dead Sea is surrounded by weird, twisted hills with ominous caves punched into them. On the waterline, you can see white ringmarks going up to the shore to show where the water level used to come to. Rather like my bathtub, in

Look Mum, no hands!

The Dead Sea. Almost impossible to drown in...

fact. The water is a dull-green, dead-looking colour. The whole place has an eerie, heavy atmosphere.

At Ein Gedi, on the shores of this strange sea, there is (believe it or not!) a health resort. All that salt is supposed to do you some good, and people have been coming here for centuries. You can't just dive in, because if you get even a tiny droplet into one of your eyes it would make peeling onions with your eyelids pale into insignficance!

The water feels soapy. When you finally get up the courage to sit down in the water, you find yourself almost lying on top of it! Your legs and feet stick out at one end, and your shoulders at the other. It's just impossible to sink, and it's really quite hard to make your legs disappear under the surface. In the Bible, Jesus once walked on the Sea of Galilee. It definitely wouldn't have been much of a miracle if he'd tried doing it here!

After a minute or two, you discover something the guide books don't tell you (you read it here first, folks!). If you have the smallest scratch, blemish or sore patch anywhere on your skin, the salty water will seek it out and give it a hard time. There are open-air showers on the beach to wash it all off.

Masada: 5-star Fortress

A few miles further south of Ein Gedi is a place with an incredible story. Masada is a flat-topped mountain overlooking the Dead Sea. Someone has said that it's like an aircraft carrier because of the way it stands on its own, away from the other mountains and hills around it.

It's the perfect place for a fortress – and that's exactly what King Herod turned it into about 30 years before Jesus was born. It was a five-star fortress, complete with swimming pool, luxury bathrooms, magnificent views, running water, VIP suites and several lifetimes' supply

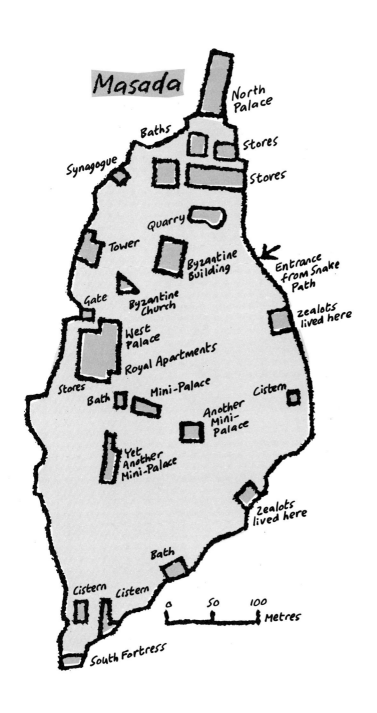

35

You'd think that a mountain miles from anywhere in the middle of the desert would be the last place to find a luxury palace. But that's exactly what was on top of Masada. This mosaic floor was once walked over by King Herod.

of food. The only thing missing was a cable car – which was added nineteen centuries after Herod.

The Cornered Rebels

In AD 66, there was a Jewish revolt in Israel, and the Romans sent their troops in to put it down. Jerusalem was completely flattened, and about 960 of the rebels took over Masada as their final hideout. The Romans pursued them and put the place to siege.

Today, you can take the cable car up to the top, or (if you've got something to prove in the machismo department) you can slog your way up the Snake Path in the blistering heat. The way up the path takes about an hour, and you should drink plenty of liquid as you climb, to prevent dehydration.

Lookout tower on Masada.

Looking down from the swaying cable car, you can see the outline of a few of the eight Roman camps on the ground far below, each in the shape of a square. It's bad enough just to stroll around Masada, the heat is so intense. But to do battle in this furnace must have been hell. The Roman commander's name was Flavius Silva, and with him was the famous 10th Legion, plus

Top Ten Sites

This is a personal choice, but I'd recommend these places as a must for getting the most out of a visit to the Holy Land. Anyway, here they are...

1 **Church of Peter's Primacy, Tabgha** (Sea of Galilee) Supremely peaceful, unspoilt, simple and very special.

2 **Church of the Annunciation** (Nazareth) This time, the church builders got it right!

3 **Garden Tomb** (Jerusalem) As a visual aid to what Jesus' death and resurrection must have been like, it can't be beaten.

4 **Masada** (Dead Sea) Overwhelming story, overwhelming place.

5 **Garden of Gethsemane** (Jerusalem) Great atmosphere both in the church and the garden itself.

6 **Wailing Wall** (Jerusalem) The powerhouse of the Jewish faith.

7 **Dome of the Rock and Temple Mount** (Jerusalem) A site holy to half the world.

8 **Dead Sea** The only swim that makes you laugh – but keep your mouth shut!

9 **Mount of Beatitudes** (Sea of Galilee) One of the best views in Israel.

10 **Capernaum** (Sea of Galilee) Galilee as Jesus saw it.

an assortment of rock-throwing, wall-battering siege engines.

Masada proved almost (but not quite) impossible to take. In the end, Silva built an enormous earth ramp up the side of the mountain to wheel his siege machine up to the walls of the fortress. You can still see the ramp. The stones thrown by the rapid-firing catapults rained down on Masada in deadly showers. Each stone weighed around 60lbs and they were painted black to make them invisible in the air until impact.

The Jewish defenders fiercely resisted, even rebuilding the wall when it was broken through. Then one evening in the spring of AD 73, the Romans finally smashed the last of the Jewish defences. They went back to their camp singing and taunting the defenders, intending to finish them off early next day.

Cheating the Romans

But the rebels decided to rob the Romans of their final victory. They burnt the town on top of Masada. The husbands embraced their wives and children, and then cut their throats. Someone wrote the names of everyone left on pieces of broken pottery, and they were put into a jar. Ten of the men were picked to kill everyone else. Once that was done, one man was chosen to kill the remaining nine, and then he fell on his own sword.

The only way the story is known was because two women and five children hid in the cellars, and escaped the slaughter. The Roman soldiers entered Masada the next morning expecting a bitter fight, but the place was dreadfully silent. The pot in which the lots were put to decide who should kill who still exists – along with some of the names.

Today Masada is respected and revered for these terrible events and for the courage that went with them. For Israelis, this is an emotive place, where all new recruits are brought to swear in allegiance to the State of Israel. 'Masada shall not fall again' is a saying among the army units, and they mean it.

Some of the rugged scenery surrounding Masada.

3 AROUND GALILEE

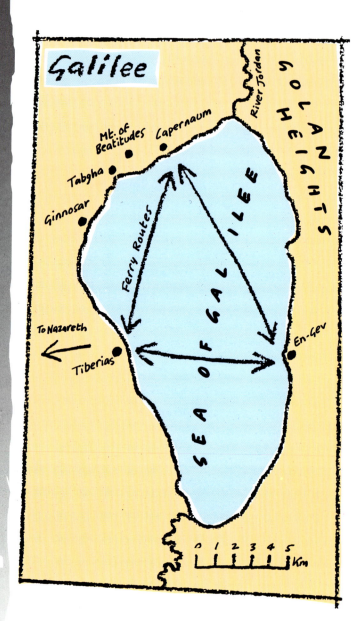

If you follow the River Jordan up from the Dead Sea, after a couple of hours' drive you arrive at the Sea of Galilee. It's not really a sea, but a large lake, and it's unlike the Dead Sea in almost every way – fresh, sparkling water, a thriving fishing industry, surrounded by green hills, etc. The only thing they have in common is that the surface of Galilee is also well below sea level. 695 feet below, in fact. That's about ten times deeper than the bottom of the North Sea.

Snapshots of Galilee

Galilee is a great place for fishing, especially around the north end of the lake. This is where the fishermen of Jesus' time used to go out to earn their living. The four Gospels (Matthew, Mark, Luke and John) are full of

The Sea of Galilee seen from Tiberias, with the ferry shuttling between here and Capernaum. Don't let looks fool you – the water can get pretty cold!

stories that happened on or around the Sea of Galilee, and when you actually come here, you can recognise the place from their snapshots. For example...

Jesus saw two boats pulled up on the beach. The fishermen had left them and were washing their nets. Jesus got into one of the boats – it belonged to Simon – and asked him to push off a little from the shore. Jesus sat in the boat and taught the crowd.

There are still fishermen on Galilee. All the restaurants around here try to serve you St Peter's fish, which is actually very bony – you spend more time piling up a little heap of bones than you do eating the thing.

Galilee Without Butlins

The amazing thing about the Sea of Galilee is that it is so quiet and peaceful. Jesus and his followers spent most of their time here, and yet the souvenir-makers and hotel-builders seem to have forgotten Galilee altogether. You won't find a 'Walking on Water Aquapark' anywhere around the lake. Although there are now fewer trees than there were, it must look very much as it did in the days when Jesus walked and sailed around here.

It's a great relief too that enormous churches haven't been built everywhere that Jesus moved in Galilee. Further south there are massive buildings that obliterate where Jesus was born and where he died. But here, the few churches that have been built are simple and uncluttered.

The Galilee that Jesus knew was a pretty prosperous area (it was good for fishing and farming) and it was much more densely populated than it is today. It's hard to believe, looking round the deserted hills, that

2,000 years ago there were many towns here with well over 10,000 people in each.

The Galileans weren't liked much by the southerners who lived down in Jerusalem. The Jerusalemites were probably a bit jealous of all the cash that sloshed around Galilee, but they also felt they were far superior. They saw the northerners as uneducated people who couldn't even speak proper (Galileans had a thick country accent).

After Jesus' temptation down near Jericho, he came up north to start his work in Galilee. On his way up, he stopped off in Nazareth, his home town, but they didn't like what he had to say to them. So Jesus carried on and settled in a fishing town called Capernaum, on the northern edge of the lake. He used this as his home from home for the next couple of years.

Tiberias – Hot on Health

On your way to Capernaum, you pass through Tiberias, which is quite a large holiday resort. This is a great place to stop and look at the Sea of Galilee, or to catch the ferry that shuttles between here and Capernaum (playing loud disco music). In the summer you can also hire pedal boats to head out into the deep waters offshore. Or if you're exceptionally brave (or just too hot) you can stand on the smooth rocks and take the plunge!

Tiberias doesn't feature much in the life of Jesus, but we do know that even then it was a popular place to come for a holiday. This was because there were hot springs here, and the place was a health spa. They didn't put you on a skimmed-milk-with-prunes diet, or expect you to jog three times around the lake before breakfast, but the hot springs were reckoned to have healing powers. So the place attracted hordes of sick people.

This is probably why Jesus was often mobbed by masses of people who wanted him to touch and heal them. If the hot springs weren't doing the trick, why not get your wheelchair over to see this local miracle-worker just a few miles away? Jesus must have been bad for business in Tiberias. The hot mineral springs are still flowing.

Tabgha's Two Churches

Travelling anti-clockwise round the lake, you come to a couple of churches off the road at a place called Tabgha (or in Greek, Heptapegon). The first church you reach sounds a bit mathematical. It's called the Church of the Multiplication. It was built in memory of the time when Jesus fed a large crowd with a few bread rolls and a couple of sardines...

When it was getting late, Jesus' disciples came to him and said, 'it is already very late and this is a lonely place. Send the people away, and let them go to the nearby farms and villages in order to buy themselves something to eat.'

So Jesus asked them, 'How much bread have you got? Go and see.' When they found out, they told him, 'Five loaves and also two fish.'

Jesus then told his disciples to make all the people divide into groups and sit down on the green grass. So the people sat down in rows, in groups of a hundred and groups of fifty. Then Jesus took the five loaves and the two fish, looked up to heaven, and gave thanks to God. He broke the loaves and gave them to his disciples to distribute to the people. He also divided the two fish among them all.

Everyone ate and had enough. Then the disciples took up twelve baskets of what was left of the bread and the fish. The number of men who were fed was five thousand.

The Church of the Multiplication was built between 1980 and 1982 on the ruins of two very ancient

The Primacy of St Peter Church on the lakeside at Tabgha. This gets the Mayo seal of approval for peacefulness.

churches. From very early times the local Christians venerated a large rock, which they believed was the actual place that Jesus broke the bread and the fish for the hungry crowd. This rock was built into the altar of the two old churches. You can still see it under the altar.

The special feature of this church is a mosaic set in the floor made in the fifth century after Christ. This

45

was only discovered in 1932, after being hidden under the rubble of the ruined church for 1,300 years. The mosaic is a kind of picture guide in stone to all the creatures and plants that live around the lake. Included in the mosaic is a basket containing five barley loaves, with two St Peter's fish, one on each side of the basket.

Rock-Steady Church

If you leave this Church and carry on along the road, you come to the entrance to the place that gets my award for being the most beautiful spot in Galilee. It's a chapel called the Primacy of St Peter. On the battered noticeboard at the gates, you are told to dress properly, and not to bring firearms into the shrine area. This small, simple church is built right at the edge of the sea, with a busy little stream running nearby.

The building is on a massive rock that runs out into the water. If you go inside (remembering to leave your machine gun outside), the rock breaks right through the wall and juts into the middle of the church. This rock has been visited by centuries of pilgrims as the place where Jesus treated his disciples to a cooked breakfast after he rose from death. We'll come back to that story later in the book.

Jesus' Sea-Stories

Outside again, the waters of the lake lap at the foot of the little black church. If you flick through the opening chapters of Matthew, Mark and Luke, this lake is a permanent backdrop to everything that happens. You get Jesus walking by the sea, teaching crowds of people from a borrowed boat. You can close your eyes and see the vast numbers of people sitting on rocks just like the ones here, listening to some of the greatest stories that Jesus told.

Which Church?

The Holy Land is littered with churches of every possible variety, run by different branches of the Christian faith. Here's a spotter's guide to a few of the more colourful species...

Greek Orthodox Characterised by colourful robes, pillar-shaped hats, clouds of incense, icons (religious paintings) and churches loaded to the gills with gold and precious stones. The Greek Orthodox have been in the Holy Land since Byzantine times. They (and other Eastern churches) celebrate Easter on a different date to Western churches.

Roman Catholic In the Holy Land, the Roman Catholic Church is represented by the Franciscans. They have been here only since the time of the Crusades. Their plumage is very plain compared to the Eastern churches. The Roman Catholic church has the Pope as its earthly leader.

Armenian This church is part of the Orthodox family of churches, from the region of Armenia (now divided between Turkey and a part of the southern USSR). They have been here since the 5th century AD.

Protestant All the varieties of Protestantism can be found in the Holy Land, from Pentecostals through to the Anglican church. With the oldest of these churches arriving only a few centuries ago, they're seen as newcomers!

Copts The Copts are the ancient Egyptian church, led at present by Pope Shenouda III from the Egyptian desert.

Abyssinians This church (also known as the Ethiopian Orthodox Church) dates back to AD 330, from Ethiopia.

And as you look out across the water, it's easy to imagine some of the events in Jesus' life connected with the lake. Here are just a few – stories originally told by Simon Peter, Jesus' follower. He actually saw them happen, somewhere out there on the sea...

47

Jesus said to Simon, 'Push your boat out further to the deep water, and you and your partners let down your nets for a catch.'

'Master,' Simon answered, 'we worked hard all night long and caught nothing. But if you say so, I will let down the nets.'

They let them down and caught such a large number of fish that the nets were about to break. So they motioned to their partners in the other boat to come and help them. They came and filled both boats so full of fish that the boats were about to sink.

When evening came, the disciples' boat was in the middle of the lake, while Jesus was alone on land. He saw that his disciples were straining at the oars, because they were rowing against the wind. So some time between three and six o'clock in the morning he came to them, walking on the water.

He was going to pass them by, but they saw him walking on the water. 'It's a ghost!' they thought, and screamed. They were all terrified when they saw him. Jesus spoke to them at once.

'Courage!' he said. 'It is I. Don't be afraid!'

Jesus the Weatherman

In the next story, there's a sudden storm on the lake. Galilee specialises in these violent storms that still whip up unexpectedly and drown people. The wind roars down a steep valley, the Valley of Pigeons, on the west side of the lake and churns the water up...

Suddenly a strong wind blew up, and the waves began to spill over into the boat, so that it was about to fill with water. Jesus was in the back of the boat, sleeping with his head on a pillow. The disciples woke him up and said, 'Teacher, don't you care that we are about to die?'

Jesus stood up and commanded the wind, 'Be quiet!' and he said to the waves, 'Be still!' The wind died down, and there was a great calm. Then Jesus said to his disciples, 'Why are you frightened? Have you still no faith?'

But they were terribly afraid and said to one another, 'Who is this man? Even the wind and waves obey him!'

This is a simulation…

The Mount of Beatitudes

If you retrace your steps from Tabgha to the Capernaum crossroads and turn right, up the hill, you eventually reach the site chosen for Jesus' Sermon on the Mount. This sermon, reported in Matthew's Gospel, contains some of the most famous words that Jesus spoke. No one knows for sure exactly *where* he preached this sermon, but Matthew tells us it was on a hillside.

The road ends just by an Italian church, donated by that well-known benefactor of the religious world – Benito Mussolini.

If you walk on past the church, and follow the path down to a large, twisted tree on the right, you're treated to a great view of the Sea of Galilee, which now lies far below you. The fields roll down to the sea, where a single fisherman is out on his boat. You can see from here why the lake is called (in Hebrew) *Chinnereth*, which means 'the harp'. This is the shape you can now see.

The meek shall inherit the earth

(but not the mineral rights)

When Jesus saw the crowds, he went up on a mountainside and sat down. His disciples came to him, and he began to teach them, saying:
'Blessed are the poor in spirit
for theirs is the kingdom of heaven.
Blessed are those who mourn,
for they will be comforted.
Blessed are the meek,
for they will inherit the earth...
You have heard that it was said, 'Love your neighbour and hate your enemy.' But I tell you: Love your enemies and pray for those who persecute you, that you may be sons of your father in heaven...
Do not worry about your life, what you will eat or drink; or about your body, what you will wear. Is not life more important than food, and the body

*more important than clothes? Look at the birds of
the air; they do not sow or reap or store away in
barns, and yet your heavenly Father feeds them.
Are you not much more valuable than they? Who
of you by worrying can add a single hour to his life?*

Keep following the path as it bends around the left,
and you reach a pile of large stones. From here you
can see right along the north shore of the lake. In the
distance is a small white church with red domes. This
is the town of Capernaum – Jesus' town. And it's
where we are going next.

Capernaum – Jesus' Borrowed Home

As you drive into the car park outside Capernaum,
there's a notice which says 'This is the town of Jesus.

*The gates into Capernaum, where Jesus lived while he was working
miracles, preaching by the lake, etc.*

Half a shekel to get in'! Capernaum was a busy fishing town back in the time of Jesus, but it's now a ruin and hasn't been lived in for hundreds of years. The ruins were bought by the Franciscans in the last century. They've dug up what is left of many of the houses, and have rebuilt some of the broken-down stonework.

It was here that Jesus began the amazing last three years of his life. He started it by calling some of the Capernaum fishermen to become his followers...

As Jesus walked along the shore of Lake Galilee, he saw two fishermen, Simon and his brother Andrew, catching fish with a net. Jesus said to them, 'Come with me, and I will teach you to catch men.' At once they left their nets and went with him.

Peter's House

From then on, Jesus made Capernaum his home town, and he lived in Simon (later called Peter) and Andrew's house. Now if you've always thought that archaeology is pretty dull stuff, read the next bit. In 1968, a couple of archaeologists were digging here and discovered the remains of Peter's house – the one that Jesus made his home.

After paying your shekel at the gate, you walk straight in to arrive right in front of Peter's house. They know that this is the right house, because ancient writers said that a church was built over the house, and there is a church matching that description built over this one. Also, in the central room of the house, Christian graffiti has been found, referring to Jesus.

Standing here, it's almost too much to take in that in this very spot Jesus taught and did some of his best-known miracles of the New Testament. Here's just one incident...

The ruins of the Jewish synagogue in Capernaum.

Jesus went back to Capernaum and the news spread that he was at home. So many people came together that there was no room left, not even out in front of the door. Jesus was preaching the message to them when four men arrived, carrying a paralysed man to Jesus. Because of the crowd, however, they could not get the man to him.

So they made a hole in the roof right above the place where Jesus was. When they had made an opening, they let the man down, lying on his mat. Seeing how much faith they had, Jesus said to the paralysed man, 'My son, your sins are forgiven.'

Jesus went on to say to the man...

'I tell you, get up, pick up your mat, and go home!' While they all watched, the man got up, picked up his mat, and hurried away. They were all completely amazed and praised God, saying, 'We have never seen anything like this!'

53

The Local Synagogue

A bit further on from Peter's house, you come to Capernaum's ancient Jewish place of worship – the synagogue. Since the early 1970s, it's been partially rebuilt. The building you can see is from the 4th century after Christ. But if you go around the side, you can see that the 4th century white stones rest on foundations made of black stone. These black stones may be the base of the synagogue that Jesus knew.

This synagogue was built by a local Roman centurion who was friendly to the Jewish people. Jesus once healed the centurion's servant, who was dying. This was where Jesus used to teach, until he angered the religious people so much that they threw him out.

These white stones date from the Capernaum synagogue that stood here some 300 years after Christ. But the black stones underneath them may well be part of the synagogue that Jesus preached in.

The trouble was that he just wasn't religious enough for them. For a start, he went to parties with some very shady characters, including prostitutes and thieves. The religious people said that he spent too much time drinking and enjoying himself. Also, he didn't behave very well on the Jewish Sabbath, when you weren't supposed to do any work. He carried on healing people, for example, which just wasn't allowed. Jesus insisted on doing these things, not to get himself a bad name, but because he wanted to meet the people who needed him most.

> *Jesus went to the synagogue and began to preach. Just then a man with an evil spirit came into the synagogue and screamed, 'What do you want with us, Jesus of Nazareth? Are you here to destroy us? I know who you are – you are God's holy messenger!'*
>
> *Jesus ordered the spirit, 'Be quiet, and come out of the man!'*
>
> *The evil spirit shook the man hard, gave a loud scream, and came out of him. The people were so amazed that they started saying to one another, 'What is this? Is it some kind of new teaching? This man has authority to give orders to the evil spirits, and they obey him!'*
>
> *And so the news about Jesus spread quickly everywhere in the province of Galilee.*

Synagogues were great places for arguments and debates about religion – and they still are. At Capernaum's synagogue, there was an American Christian coach party sitting at one end of the building, being shown around by their Jewish tour guide. They began to debate with their guide on why he was a Jew, rather than a Christian.

The argument went on for some time, and then ended in laughter when the guide said, 'It's amazing to

Some of the amazing carvings from the Capernaum synagogue.

think that Jesus probably had exactly these same arguments with the local Jews in this very synagogue, 2,000 years ago!'

We leave the sleepy ruins that saw so much activity in the time of Jesus, and head south towards our next stop – Jerusalem.

The Most Destroyed Place

About an hour and a half from Galilee, travelling via Nazareth, is a place that has fascinated people for centuries. It holds as much fascination today, because of its name – Megiddo (or in Hebrew, *Armageddon*). The place is actually a large mound, where more than 20 cities have been built and destroyed in battle. From the 30th century BC, hundreds of thousands of people have died here.

Megiddo looks out over a vast plain called the Valley of Jezreel. In ancient times it was a strategic fort, guarding the whole area. On the hill today you can poke around the ruins and see (among other things) palaces and stables that King David and Solomon must have known. There's also a deep tunnel which used to be Megiddo's water supply. You can follow the tunnel all the way out at the bottom of the hill.

Where Jesus Walked

Here's a list of the major authentic sites you can visit connected with Jesus...

- **Church of the Nativity, Bethlehem** (Jesus' birthplace)
- **Sea of Galilee** (The territory Jesus knew)
- **Capernaum** (Jesus made it his home)
- **Mount Hermon** (Where Jesus was transfigured)
- **Mount of Olives** (Jesus' entry into Jerusalem, site of his ascension)
- **Temple Mount** (Jesus taught here in his last days)
- **Gabbatha** (The Roman Pavement where he was condemned)
- **Golgotha** (Place of crucifixion either in Church of the Holy Sepulchre, or Skull Hill)
- **The Tomb** (Site of the resurrection either in Holy Sepulchre or the Garden Tomb)

Armageddon is a symbol in the Bible for the final conflict between the forces of good and evil. It's still talked about as the place where the ultimate, apocalyptic battle will be fought at the end of time. This idea comes from a passage near the end of the Bible...

Then the sixth angel poured out his bowl on the great river Euphrates. The river dried up, to provide a way for the kings who come from the east. Then I saw three unclean spirits that looked like frogs. They were coming out of the mouth of the dragon, the mouth of the beast, and the mouth of the false prophet. They are the spirits of demons that perform miracles. These three spirits go out to all the kings of the world, to bring them together for the battle on the great Day of Almighty God...

Then the spirits brought the kings together in the place that in Hebrew is called Armageddon.

Then the seventh angel poured out his bowl in the air. A loud voice came from the throne in the temple, saying,'It is done!' There were flashes of lightning, rumblings and peals of thunder, and a terrible earthquake... The great city was split into three parts, and the cities of all countries were destroyed.

4 INTO JERUSALEM

The last week of Jesus' life was spent in Jerusalem, and it's this final week that Christians remember at Easter. For Jesus, the week began in a dramatic way, as he and his followers approached the city from Jericho, coming over the Mount of Olives. Thousands of other pilgrims were also on the road to Jerusalem at the time, because the highlight of the Jewish year, the Passover festival, was about to begin. The Bible records what happened...

> The next day the large crowd that had come to the Passover Festival heard that Jesus was coming to Jerusalem. So they took branches of palm-trees and went out to meet him, shouting, 'Praise God! God bless him who comes in the name of the Lord! God bless the King of Israel!'
> Jesus found a donkey and rode on it, just as the Scripture says,
> 'Do not be afraid, city of Zion!
> Here comes your king,
> riding on a young donkey.'

Pilgrim's Eye-View

If you want to see the best view of Jerusalem, then the Mount of Olives is really the place to come. This is the first place pilgrims traditionally visit when coming to Jerusalem. You turn sharp left by the garage at the north-east corner of the city walls, and head towards the Intercontinental Hotel. There's a large parking area in front of the hotel at the top of the mount, which gives you a panoramic view of the Old City.

Separating you from the city is the Kidron Valley, with its many Jewish and Muslim cemeteries and tombs. We'll come back to these in a moment. Then there is the city wall itself, built from honey-coloured stone. Behind the wall is a great paved area called the Temple Mount, which is where the Jewish Temple

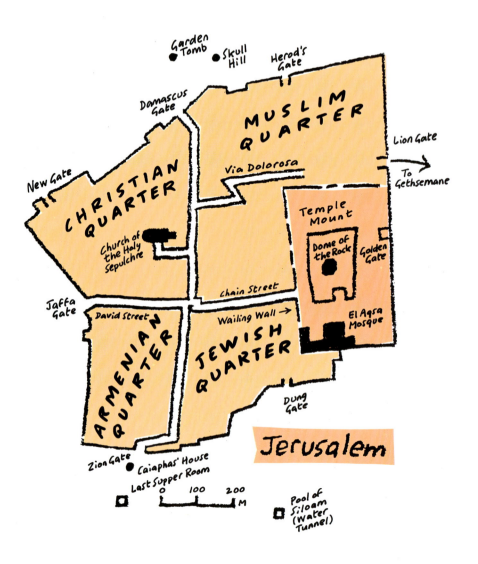

Jerusalem

stood in the time of Jesus, and where King Solomon, almost 3,000 years ago, built the first Jewish Temple.

On the Temple Mount there now stands the Dome of the Rock. In the winter it can be very cold here, with occasional snow, rain, or a freezing wind. But on a hot summer's day, the dome flashes in the sun, and it's

Modern Jerusalem

Old Jerusalem today is divided into four Quarters. These are the Christian, the Muslim, the Jewish and the Armenian Quarters. the last two are particularly interesting as areas of the city…

- The **Armenian Quarter** is walled off from the rest of the Old City, so that it's really a city within a city. The gate into it is shut early every evening, just as used to happen for all four quarters. It's worth visiting to see the Church of St James and the Armenian Museum.

- The **Jewish Quarter** is only to be entered cautiously, on foot and with very modest dress! Look out for men wearing pin-striped robes and broad-brimmed black hats with white skull caps peeping out under the back. These are ultra-Orthodox Jews. This is a strictly Jewish neighbourhood, where the Jewish Law is observed down to the last full stop. Don't be seen clicking a camera shutter here on the sabbath – it would be seen as *work* , and will get you into trouble.

Jerusalem is a living city, not just a museum exhibit. In many places the skyline is crammed with modern buildings.

61

easily the first thing about this view that catches your eye. This is the religious focus for Jerusalem's Muslims.

If you look down to the left of where the wall ends, there is a small, flattish hill, with some rather run-down looking buildings on it. This is the Hill of Ophel, where Jerusalem was originally built after King David had captured it (David was Solomon's father). Since those days, the city has moved up the hill to the north.

In the heart of the walled city, you can see the domes and towers of churches, and many Muslim minarets, from which Muslims are called to prayer five times each day. These are reminders that Jerusalem is sacred to Christianity and Islam, as well as to Judaism.

Beyond all the ancient bits, you can see the skyscrapers, hotels and cranes that mark modern Jerusalem. So the view from the Mount of Olives is very much a mixture of the old and the new.

There's a rumour that this view of the city was felt to be 'not quite right' by some of the American tourists staying in the Intercontinental Hotel. Apparently the Dome of the Rock wasn't in the best place for viewing from the hotel, and they asked if the Dome could be moved across to correct things...

God's City

Standing here with the city spread out before you, it's not surprising to know that the Jewish people have something approaching a love affair with the old place. Centuries before the time of Jesus, they saw Jerusalem as a symbol of all their hopes and dreams.

Sadly, Jerusalem hasn't been a very peaceful place since then. It's probably seen more bloodshed over the years than any other city in the world. It's been besieged by the armies of ancient Babylon, the

Romans, the Turks, the Arabs… you name it, they've been here. But this seems only to have strengthened Jewish love for Jerusalem.

Way back when the Jews were exiled in Babylon, with Jerusalem in ruins, one exile said it all…

Those who captured us told us to sing;
they told us to entertain them:
'Sing us a song about Zion.
How can we sing a song to the Lord
in a foreign land?
May I never be able to play the harp again
if I forget you, Jerusalem!
May I never be able to sing again
if I do not remember you,
if I do not think of you as my greatest joy!

Zion, by the way, is another name given to the city.

Beware of Camels!

This viewing area is very popular with the tourists and pilgrims which also makes it popular with some of the local Arabs who want to relieve you of some of your cash. There are usually a few locals with a camel on the Mount of Olives. Everything is very friendly, until the camel 'accidentally' wanders into the background of a picture you're taking. You have to watch out because this can be chargeable!

How about trying a kick-start?

Even worse is if you are persuaded to sit on the camel for a picture. One tourist who thought the owners were just being friendly sat down for the shot when suddenly the camel got to its feet, lumbered a few paces, broke wind, and then sat down again. Things turned a bit ugly when the tourist refused to pay £20 for the 'camel ride' he'd just been given!

Mayo meets Jacko. The donkey's name (according to its owner) is 'Michael Jackson'. Have the operations gone too far?

Churches, Churches, Churches

If you like churches, then you'll like the Mount of Olives. If not, then your best bet is to view the city and then beat a retreat back down the hill again. It seems as if there's a church here for almost every time that Jesus coughed. This is also true for Jerusalem as a whole. It's not called 'the Holy City' for nothing. The place is packed so full of synagogues, mosques and churches, it's amazing that there's any room left for people to live.

The trend of covering holy sites with churches begins here, on the Mount of Olives. There's the Pater Noster Church, just down from the Intercontinental Hotel, where Jesus is believed to have taught his disciples the Lord's prayer. The prayer itself is carved onto the walls in 60 different languages.

One of the most famous sights of Jerusalem – the Dome of the Rock standing on the place where the Jewish Temple stood in ancient times.

Then there's the Chapel of the Ascension, marking the site of Jesus' last footprint on earth. This chapel is actually Muslim, as Christians aren't the only ones to revere Jesus. The major difference is that the Muslims see Jesus as a prophet, while Christians worship him as the only Son of God. Inside the octagonal chapel is a rock with a footprint in it.

You can also visit Dominus Flevit (latin for 'the Lord wept'). This church with a tower roof in the shape of tears is said to mark the spot where Jesus looked down on Jerusalem and wept over it. He cried because he foresaw the destruction that would come to the city only 40 years after his death…

Jesus came closer to the city, and when he saw it, he wept over it, saying, 'If you only knew

*today what is needed for peace! But now you
cannot see it! The time will come when your
enemies will surround you with barricades,
blockade you, and close in on you from every
side. They will completely destroy you and the
people within your walls; not a single stone will
they leave in its place, because you did not
recognise the time when God came to save you!*

This is exactly what the Roman troops did to
Jerusalem. We'll be looking at those events in more
detail in the section on the Wailing Wall.

There's also the Russian Church of Mary Magdalene,
famous for its onion domes. And as if all that wasn't
enough, you'll be glad to know that a new church, the
Church of the Holy Heart, is under construction!

It's not always boiling hot in Jerusalem. It's even been known to <u>snow</u>...

The Golden Gate

Before coming down from the top of the Mount of Olives, there's one last detail to see. In the city wall below the Temple Mount is a large, walled-up double gate, called the Golden Gate. It was built some time between 450 and 600 years after Christ, and was walled up by Suleiman the Magnificent (the Turkish Sultan) in 1530. It has never been reopened. Suleiman, by the way, was the guy who built most of the walls around the Old City that you can see today.

Legend has it that the Messiah will enter Jerusalem by this gate at the end of time, and that it will stay closed until then. According to Jewish belief, the Messiah will set up two bridges between the gate and the Mount of Olives: one made of iron, the other made of paper. Everyone (the living and the dead) will have to cross the deep valley by the bridge of his or her choice. Unpredictably, the iron bridge will collapse (showing that you can't rely on what *appears* to be strong), while the paper bridge gets you across in one piece. So much for cast-iron guarantees.

All this explains the popularity for having your grave on the Mount of Olives. Good Jews and Muslims want to be in on the action as and when it happens.

Whether the legends are proved true or not, the Golden Gate and the Mount of Olives are strongly connected with Jesus the Messiah. It's very likely that this gate is built over the ruins of the gate Jesus used to enter Jerusalem from the Mount of Olives. And it was from the Mount of Olives that Jesus ascended into heaven following his resurrection.

One final thing. The shutting-up of the Golden Gate was predicted by the Old Testament prophet Ezekiel, 2,000 years before it happened. In a vision of the city, he was taken to see the gate…

The man led me to the outer gate at the east side of the temple area. The gate was closed, and the Lord said to me, 'This gate will stay closed and will never be opened. No human being is allowed to use it, because I, the Lord God of Israel, have entered through it.'

Jerusalem Today

If Jesus and his disciples were to take a bus around Jerusalem today, there is virtually nothing they would recognise from the city they knew. Perhaps the shape of the hills would be familiar, but even these have changed. There used to be a 90-foot deep valley running right through the city, with bridges crossing it, but this is now completely filled with rubbish and rubble from the many times the city has been razed to the ground.

The local cuisine – not always the temptation it's cracked up to be!

One ancient site you <u>mustn't</u> miss.

The Old City (inside the Turkish walls) is now about 30 feet higher than it was when Jesus was here. This is because it's easier to build *on top of* demolished buildings than to clear away the ruins first. So with each demolition, the city has grown a bit taller. You can see this difference in heights dramatically at the Damascus Gate. If you stand outside the gate and look down to the left, you'll see a more ancient, smaller gate, half-sunk in the earth. This gate was built by the Romans, soon after the time of Jesus.

Another massive change, of course, is that Jerusalem is now much bigger than the Old City. The city has developed rapidly since the State of Israel was born in 1948. Whole new neighbourhoods have grown mainly to the west of the Old City, together with

The Damascus Gate leading into the Old City. This is one of Jerusalem's busiest gates.

University campuses, hotels, fast-food restaurants, and so on.

Talking of fast-food restaurants, no visit to Jerusalem is complete without a look-in at MacDavid's, which sells hamburgers almost as good as McYou-Know-Who, all washed down with lavish helpings of kosher-kola. It's on the right as you go up the Jaffa road away from the city walls. The trouble is that eating out in Israel can be unbelievably expensive. Perhaps the massive VAT on food has something to do with it...

A Stroll in the Suq

What is Jerusalem like at ground-level? A first walk into the Old City feels very strange. Like taking a

The Jaffa Road is a typically busy road in Jerusalem.

Two old friends stop for a chat on a Jerusalem street.

Street-sellers. Haggling over prices is what it's all about.

Jerusalem's Via Dolorosa, lined with shops selling everything from fruit and veg to religious souvenirs…

The Via Dolorosa as it climbs one of the hills inside Jerusalem.

You see lots of these in Jerusalem. Cameras that is!

Jerusalem street-life.

Jerusalem's Jaffa Road.

journey back in time. For a start, you enter the city through one of its seven open gates. The streets are narrow, descending by steps into the ancient valleys of the city.

Nine-tenths of Jerusalem is a pedestrian precinct, mostly only a few feet wide, lined with small cavern-like shops, tiny dark windows high up the walls and low doorways into unexpected courtyards. This is the Jerusalem suq, where the narrow market streets are choked with crowds wanting to buy, or just wanting to push their way through. All the time, shop owners call out to you to come and see what they are selling, and small kids run around with cheap jewellery or postcards, badgering you almost to death for a few shekels.

In the tiny shops you can buy Arab head-dresses, Jewish stars of David, crosses of every shape, size and colour, stuffed camels, clay oil lamps, olive-wood carvings, rosaries, ancient coins, ancient books and ancient-looking food. Your nose is bombarded by a bewildering menu of smells – some of which are very bitter and not at all tempting. And then there are the sweets – the 'full of eastern promise' variety. The entire city must have dental problems because if all the sweets were laid out side by side, they would add up to several acres of sugar.

In some of the wider places are street-sellers offering you Jerusalem's speciality – falafels. These are spiced chick peas stuffed with – no, it's indescribable. And anyway, this isn't a cookbook. It's enough to say that not every falafel you can buy on the street is all that good for you. According to some of the Israeli soldiers patrolling the city's streets, before you buy your falafel, it's a good idea to know the way to the hospital – by the *shortest* route!

The military are everywhere, women as well as men, with guns casually slung over their shoulders.

For westerners, this can be a bit of a shock. You can sometimes see young women going for a night out in Jerusalem, dressed up, but each of them carrying a rifle.

As you walk through the suq, every now and then a small flock of sheep is driven past you, or a miniature, souped-up tractor roars down the steps, crowds or not. The suq can feel rather threatening at first to the average westerner – but generally it's pretty safe. Apparently it's *not* a good idea for women to walk around alone (especially if they're dressed to kill – or even just to maim). And walking through certain areas at night isn't normally the sign of a high IQ.

The Temple Mount

If you have ever seen any pictures of Jerusalem, or if someone has sent you a postcard from there, the chances are that it will include a shot of this area. To Jews and Christians it's called the Temple Mount. The Muslims who own it call it Haram esh-Sharif. The whole area is closed to non-Muslims on Fridays, during the Muslim holy day, and during special festivals.

For different reasons, the vast, flat site (engineered by King Herod the Great) is holy to Jews, Christians and Muslims. Here they are in a nutshell…

King
Solomon

● For Jews, this is the place where the Temple stood, on and off, for about 1,000 years. The Temple, first built by King Solomon (renowned for his wisdom and his 1,000 women), was the focus of the Jewish faith. The Ark of the Covenant and the 10 Commandments were kept here.

● For Christians, this is where Jesus taught during the last few days before he was crucified. He taught in the Temple that was being rebuilt by King Herod.

73

● For Muslims, this is No. 3 in their Holiest Places Chart. It ranks after Mecca and Medina. The Temple Mount is holy as the place where Abraham tried to sacrifice his son Isaac, and because Muhammed ascended into heaven from here by night.

In the past, this site has been more important to Jews and Muslims than to Christians. And it's still a red-hot issue in relations between Jews and Arabs. Herod's Temple was destroyed by the Romans in AD 70, and has never been rebuilt. Since about AD 700, the Temple Mount has been in Muslim hands (apart from one short break). Although Israeli soldiers guard the gates into the site, you won't find any Jews inside – this is strictly Muslim territory.

Some Jewish groups are very unhappy that their government decided to keep the Temple Mount Muslim. There have been plots to blow up the Dome of the Rock, to reclaim the holy site for Judaism, and even some plans to rebuild the Temple. On the other side, this site can act as a focus for Muslim discontent. The Dome of the Rock was recently tear-gassed by Israeli soldiers who suspected that terrorists were hiding inside.

Flashback to the Year Dot

In the Year Dot (the time of Christ) things weren't much different here. The Romans actually built a massive fortress right next to the Temple so that they could look down on it and send in the riot squads at the first whiff of trouble.

When Jesus arrived in the Temple, the day after he rode over the Mount of Olives on his donkey, he almost stirred up a riot, and he was pretty fortunate not to get arrested. He found the Temple courtyards full of 'honest harry' street-sellers. You know the type:

'I'm not here to *cheat* you– I'm here to *treat* you!' When Jesus saw it all, he wasn't just angry...

> *Jesus began to drive out all those who were buying and selling. He overturned the tables of money-changers and the stools of those who sold pigeons, and he would not let anyone carry anything through the temple courtyards.*
>
> *He then taught the people: 'It is written in the Scriptures that God said, "My Temple will be called a house of prayer for the people of all nations." But you have turned it into a hideout for thieves!'*

It wasn't a good start to the week. And as the countdown to Jesus' crucifixion ticked on, the friction between Jesus and his enemies in the Temple (the Pharisees) got steadily worse. They tried to trip him up with trick questions, and he ripped them to shreds in front of the people visiting the Temple. It was here, in some corner of this massive Temple area, that Jesus insulted his enemies (in the worst possible taste)...

> *You hypocrites! You are like whitewashed tombs, which look fine on the outside but are full of bones and decaying corpses on the inside. In the same way, on the outside you appear good to everybody, but inside you are full of hypocrisy and sins.*

It was around this time that Jesus' enemies decided that he was becoming very dangerous and needed to be silenced. For good. But they couldn't get rid of Jesus on their own. They had to have the help of one of his followers. It had to be an *inside* job.

Meanwhile, Jesus carried on speaking in the Temple, telling parables, denouncing the religious leaders, healing people, and so on. Jesus' enemies tried to have one more go with their trick questions. This has to be one of the most dramatic stories from Jesus' life...

Early the next morning Jesus went back to the Temple. All the people gathered round him, and he sat down and began to teach them. The teachers of the Law and the Pharisees brought in a woman who had been caught committing adultery, and they made her stand before them all.

'Teacher' they said to Jesus, 'this woman was caught in the very act of committing adultery. In our Law Moses commanded that such a woman be stoned to death. Now, what do you say?' They said this to trap Jesus, so that they could accuse him. But he bent over and wrote on the ground with his finger.

As they stood there asking him questions, he straightened himself up and said to them, 'Whichever one of you has committed no sin may throw the first stone at her.' Then he bent over again and wrote on the ground. When they heard this, they all left, one by one, the older ones first. Jesus was left alone, with the woman still standing there. He straightened himself up and said to her, 'Where are they? Is there no one left to condemn you?'

'No one, sir,' she answered.

'Well then,' Jesus said, ' I do not condemn you either. Go, but do not sin again.'

The Dome of the Rock

There are ten gates entering the Temple Mount from the Old City. It's a relief to emerge from the narrow maze of the Jerusalem alleys and suddenly find yourself out in this light, open space. The Mount covers about 35 acres and right smack in the middle is the Dome of the Rock. This is the world's oldest mosque – and it's been standing here for 1,300 years.

The exterior of the Dome of the Rock is covered in thousands of brightly-coloured tiles. These are formed into geometric patterns and inscriptions from the Muslim holy book, the Koran.

The mosque is octagonal, and is topped by what looks like a golden dome, but is actually made from aluminium and bronze. Originally it was said to be overlaid by 10,000 sheets of pure gold. Below the dome, the outside walls are covered in intricately-designed mosaics.

77

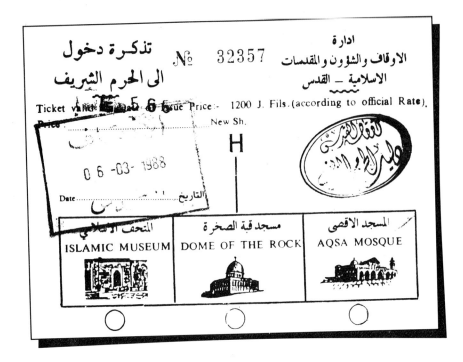

For a few shekels, you can buy a ticket that allows you into the Dome of the Rock, the neighbouring El Aqsa Mosque and the Islamic Museum. You have to leave your shoes outside before going in. The first surprise is that the place is carpeted. The carpets smell a bit from all those feet, but they're supposed to be extremely valuable. The second surprise is the massive, rough rock that fills the centre of the mosque.

Standing inside, the sun blazes through the beautiful stained-glass. The interesting features are connected with the story of Muhammed. The Prophet took a night-time ride on a flying horse from here, and as he ascended, the rock itself tried to follow him on his journey up. The Archangel Gabriel (who we last met in Nazareth) averted a serious incident by physically holding the mountain down. It's tough work being an archangel. His fingerprints and Muhammed's footprint can be seen in the rock.

You can also go into a cave underneath the rock (yes, it's *another* holy site with its own cave), where the dead are reported to come to pray twice a week.

If you go round the back of the Dome of the Rock, there is a smaller version of it, called the Dome of the Chain. This was used as an architect's model for the real thing, and as a giant money-box to keep the contributions that were used to built the Dome of the Rock.

The Wailing Wall

Just over the wall from the all-Arab Temple Mount is the all-Jewish Western Wall (famous throughout the world as the 'Wailing Wall'). This is the holiest site in the world for all Jews, and must be *the* most unusual place of worship anywhere. The wall is all that the Romans left of Herod's Temple when they conquered and demolished Jerusalem forty years after the crucifixion of Jesus.

In the terrible destruction, the Roman troops became uncontrollable after all the months of trying to break through the walls to capture the city. They set fire to the Temple, butchered a large proportion of the Jewish population, and took away the Jewish homeland. This was one of the greatest catastrophes in Jewish history, rivalled only by the holocaust under Hitler, when 6 million Jews were systematically killed. The Jews had no land to call their own between the Roman destruction of Jerusalem and this century.

Jews have come to this wall for hundreds of years to mourn over the destruction and the persecution they have suffered. In 1967, when Israeli paratroopers captured this part of the city from the Jordanians, the Jewish people were able to call this site their own for the first time in 1,900 years. A large open space was created in front of the wall, which was renamed the Western Wall.

The massive blocks in the first five layers of the wall are what is left of Herod's Temple wall. Incredibly,

Dwarfed by these ancient stones, Jews gather at the Western (or 'Wailing')
Wall to pray.

there are 19 more layers of these stones going down
beneath your feet. On top of Herod's stones are four
layers of Roman masonry. Everything on top of that is
'recent' – only a *few* centuries old!

Women go to the right and men to the left to stand
facing the wall to pray. The women are meant to pray
on their own, quietly. But the men gather in large

groups and are allowed to make a noise. As you approach the wall, you are given a cardboard skull-cap to cover your head. An amazing variety of Jewish people come here to pray – wearing long black coats, trilbys or big, bushy hats. Some of them have long beards with ringlets at the side of their heads falling down. They all pray in the same way, rocking and swaying as they chant. Some of them repeatedly nod their heads at the wall.

The whole place is really an open-air synagogue, with the massive stones of King Herod looking down on it all. Each crack and gap in the stones is jammed full of little pieces of paper. These are written-out prayers and requests to God, and because of them, the Wailing Wall has been called 'God's Postbox'.

Three Holy Days

Because Jerusalem is a city with three religions (Jewish, Christian and Muslim), there are no less than three holy days in every seven! You'd have thought they could all have agreed to keep the same day, but religions don't work like that. Here they are, in turn...

Friday is holy to the Muslims. Shops and businesses close for the day, so it's no use trying to go shopping in the Muslim Quarter of the city. On Fridays, the Temple Mount is closed to all non-Muslims, while Muslims go to worship.

Saturday is the Jewish shabat (sabbath). Actually, this starts on Friday night at sunset, and ends at the same time on Saturday. In the Jewish Quarter the sabbath is *strictly* observed, and should you be stupid enough to drive a car into this part of the city, you can expect to have stones thrown at it. The main point of the Jewish sabbath is not to do work. Even turning on a light or pushing a button is classified as work, so in good Jewish hotels there are sabbath lifts that stop at every floor to save people from breaking the holy day!

Sunday is the Christian holy day. Shops in the Christian Quarter are closed, and some interesting places (for example, the stone pavement under the Convent of the Sisters of Zion) are closed all day, too.

5 ONE JERUSALEM NIGHT

This Chapter's Hit List...

Coenaculum

Garden of Gethsemane

Basilica of the Agony

St Peter in Gallicantu

Valley of Hinnom

Hezekiah's Tunnel

On the south side of Jerusalem, just outside the city walls, is a place called Mount Zion. The city walls once used to enclose this part of the city too. On Mount Zion there is an old church building, the Coenaculum, that claims to be the place where Jesus and his disciples ate their final meal together – the Last Supper.

Frankly, it isn't very convincing! The hall where it is all supposed to have happened was built by the Crusaders, and it looks very much like a well-preserved room from a solid English castle. If this *is* the site of the Last Supper, then the room Jesus ate in must have been completely destroyed long ago.

Zeroing in on Jesus

The Last Supper probably took place in the upstairs room of a house owned by John Mark – he and his mother were friends of Jesus. This room is tradition-ally known as the Upper Room, which is the name given to it in the Bible. It was the Jewish feast of Passover in Jerusalem, and Jesus wanted to celebrate the traditional Passover meal with his friends quietly.

Jesus knew that his enemies in Jerusalem were already plotting his death and were looking for ways to arrest him. He also knew that this was going to be difficult for them. The problem was that Jesus was very popular. He was spending every day in the Temple, teaching the crowds, healing the sick and so on. If they tried to arrest him in front of these people, there would be a riot.

That left the night-time to arrest him. But this was also next to impossible. Jerusalem was *heaving* with the thousand of pilgrims who had come up to the city for Passover. They all had to sleep somewhere, and most of them stuck up tents around the Mount of Olives, turning the place into a sort of giant campsite. Finding

Jesus and his friends after dark in all that would be like searching for a pork pie at a Jewish wedding.

The only way they could get to Jesus was to find someone to betray him, someone who could say exactly where he would be during the night. And some time during that final week, they found their man. His name was Judas.

Then Judas Iscariot, one of the twelve disciples, went off to the chief priests in order to betray Jesus to them. They were pleased to hear what he had to say, and promised to give him money. So Judas started looking for a good chance to hand Jesus over to them.

Condemned Man's Last Meal

Because of the plots, Jesus arranged the place for his final meal with the disciples secretly. He didn't want his last few hours with them disturbed. In the secret Upper Room, after they'd finished eating, Jesus gave the disciples bread and wine to symbolise his body and his blood. He broke the bread, to show that his body would be broken, and poured out the wine, to show that his blood would be spilt. Christians still remember Jesus' death by eating bread and wine.

During the evening, Jesus suddenly announced that one of the disciples was going to betray him…

When it was evening, Jesus and the twelve disciples sat down to eat. During the meal Jesus said, 'I tell you, one of you will betray me.'

The disciples were very upset and began to ask him, one after the other, 'Surely, Lord, you don't mean me?'

Jesus answered,'One who dips his bread in the dish with me will betray me. The Son of Man will die as the Scriptures say he will, but how terrible for that man who betrays the Son of Man!

It would have been better for that man if he had never been born!'

Judas, the traitor, spoke up. 'Surely, Teacher, you don't mean me?' he asked.

Jesus answered, 'So you say.'

While they were eating, Jesus took a piece of bread, gave a prayer of thanks, broke it, and gave it to his disciples. 'Take and eat it, ' he said. 'This is my body.'

Then he took a cup, gave thanks to God, and gave it to them. 'Drink it, all of you,' he said. 'This is my blood, which seals God's covenant, my blood poured out for many for the forgiveness of sins...'

Then they sang a hymn and went out to the Mount of Olives.

The Basilica of the Agony, Gethsemane. In this garden, just by the city walls of Jerusalem, Jesus was betrayed by Judas to his enemies.

Garden of Gethsemane

The walk from the Upper Room to the Garden of Gethsemane is actually very short. You go down a very steep hill around the side of the old walls, across the Kidron Valley (overshadowed by the Mount of Olives) and there you are. This is the journey that Jesus and eleven of his disciples made on the Thursday night before the first Good Friday.

Outside the wall into the garden are the words 'Here Jesus began his passion. Suffered, sweated blood.' Inside is a pathway that goes around the garden, which has a number of olive trees still growing in it. Some of these trees are centuries old, and one or two may have been young at the time Jesus was here. At the very least, they are reckoned to be descended from the trees

These trees in the Garden of Gethsemane are probably descended from the ones which Jesus prayed under before his arrest.

here at the time. It's very easy to imagine what the place must have been like then.

It was here that Jesus spent his last hour of freedom. As he thought through the terrible ordeal that was fast approaching, he went through terrible anguish. Luke, one of the Gospel writers, says that 'his sweat was like drops of blood falling to the ground'. While his close friends (Peter, James and John) kept dropping off to sleep through exhaustion, Jesus prayed here that he wouldn't have to go through all the agonies ahead. When he had finished praying, Judas arrived with an armed guard. Jesus and the disciples had often come to this garden, and Judas knew that he could find them here…

Jesus threw himself face downwards on the ground, and prayed, 'My Father, if it is possible, take this cup of suffering from me! Yet not what I want, but what you want…'

Then he returned to the disciples and said, 'Are you still sleeping and resting? Look! The hour has come for the Son of Man to be handed over to the power of sinful men. Get up, let us go. Look, here is the man who is betraying me!'

Jesus was still speaking when Judas, one of the twelve disciples, arrived. With him was a large crowd armed with swords and clubs and sent by the chief priests and the elders. The traitor had given the crowd a signal: 'The man I kiss is the one you want. Arrest him!'

Judas went straight to Jesus and said, 'Peace be with you, Teacher,' and kissed him.

Jesus answered, 'Be quick about it, friend!'

Then they came up, arrested Jesus, and held him tight. One of those who were with Jesus drew his sword and struck at the High Priest's slave, cutting off his ear. 'Put your sword back in its place,' Jesus said to him. 'All who take the sword will die by the sword…'

Then Jesus spoke to the crowd. 'Did you have to come with swords and clubs to capture me, as though I were an outlaw? Every day I sat down and taught in the Temple, and you did not arrest me. But all this has happened in order to make what the prophets wrote in the Scriptures come true.' Then all the disciples left him and ran away.

Today, the Garden of Gethsemane has a church alongside it called the Basilica of the Agony (alias the Church of All Nations). It's a modern church, built in 1924 by the same architect who built the Church of Dominus Flevit, further up the Mount of Olives. The church next to the garden is really worth going into for a few quiet moments. The atmosphere inside really captures the whole mood of Jesus' agony and betrayal.

One of the sculptures at Yad Vashem, the memorial to the six million Jewish victims of Hitler's holocaust between 1933 and 1945. Yad Vashem houses many documents, letters and photographs from the Nazi era.

Rough Justice

From Gethsemane, Jesus was probably taken back the way he came to the house of Caiaphas, the High Priest, which was near the Upper Room. The Church of St Peter in Gallicantu (which means St Peter at the Cock's Crow) is now said to stand over the remains of Caiaphas's house. The ruins include what might be the courtroom where Jesus was tried, the prison he was held in, and a condemned prisoner's cell at the bottom of the building.

In the early hours of Good Friday morning Jesus was dragged before the Jewish Council, who had been called for an urgent meeting at Caiaphas's House. His enemies were hell-bent on having him put to death. They brought in a load of people who were prepared to accuse anyone for the right amount of shekels, and they told all the lies they'd been paid for. Unfortunately, their stories about Jesus contradicted each other.

But then the High Priest stepped in...

The High Priest stood up in front of them all and questioned Jesus...'Are you the Messiah, the Son the the Blessed God?'

'I am,' answered Jesus, 'and you will all see the Son of Man seated on the right of the Almighty and coming with the clouds of heaven!'

The High Priest tore his robes and said, 'We don't need any more witnesses! You heard his blasphemy. What is your decision?'

They all voted against him: he was guilty and should be put to death.

Some of them began to spit on Jesus, and they blindfolded him and hit him. 'Guess who hit you!' they said. And the guards took him, and slapped him.

The Fatal Cock-Crow

From then on, Jesus' fate was sealed. The Jewish Council couldn't legally put someone to death – only the Roman authorities could do that. But the religious leaders knew that they would be able to persuade Pontius Pilate, the Roman Governor, to do what they wanted.

While Jesus was inside being condemned to death, one of Jesus' disciples was outside the house, watching to see what would happen, warming himself by a fire in the courtyard. It was Peter. At the Last Supper, Jesus had told Peter that before the cock crowed twice, Peter would have denied three times that he even knew Jesus. Peter had been angry at Jesus for saying it.

As he stood outside, a servant-girl recognised Peter as one of Jesus' disciples. Peter denied it. She then told the other people standing around – and again Peter said he wasn't Jesus' follower. But then someone in the crowd helpfully pointed out that Peter had an accent from Galilee – so he *must* be from Jesus' group...

Then Peter said,'I swear that I am telling the truth! May God punish me if I am not! I do not know the man you are talking about!'
Just then a cock crowed a second time, and Peter remembered how Jesus had said to him, 'Before the cock crows twice, you will say three times that you do not know me.' and he broke down and cried.

Dustbin Valley

Leaving the story of Jesus for a moment, one place that's interesting to look at in the area of St Peter's church is the Valley of Hinnom. This is a very steep gorge that runs around the south of the Old City. In ancient times this was Jerusalem's rubbish dump, in the days before bottle banks and black plastic bags. The valley was usually full of smoke, as the rubbish was always being burned here. Because of these fires, the valley gave its name to *Gehenna* – the Greek name for hell.

Down in the valley, there's a surprise. It's *still* an unofficial rubbish tip, with white plastic bags bulging with Jerusalem rubbish thrown down the slopes. If you carry on into the delapidated Arab areas south of the city, make sure that your car doesn't have yellow number plates. (In modern-day Israel, yellow number plates show you are from Israeli areas. Blue number plates are Palestinian.)

This valley is a pretty unhappy place. In Old Testament days, when Israel had rebelled against God to follow the fierce, local religions, child-sacrifice went on down here. And at the bottom of the valley is a

This photo is taken from the soon-to-be-published book, 101 Things to do with A Stale Bagel.

90

Is It Kosher?

Jews who are serious about their faith will eat only kosher food (food that is pure according to Jewish diet laws). A visit to Israel makes you aware of what this means in at least two ways...

Meat Some different meats aren't allowed for example, pork (so forget a breakfast of *bacon* and eggs!), game and shellfish. These were ruled out right at the beginning of Israels' history, because of their tendency to go bad in a hot climate.

Dairy Products In a kosher restaurant or hotel, dairy products can't be mixed with meat. So if you had a hamburger, you wouldn't be able to follow it up with a milkshake and you wouldn't be allowed any butter on your baked potato! This need to keep milk and meat completely separate is taken very seriously. Some Jewish hotels have *two* kitchens, one to handle the meat, the other the milk foods.

place called Haceldama, 'the field of Blood'. It was this field that Judas bought with the money he was paid to betray Jesus. He bought it for one simple reason – to hang himself from one of the trees. It's hardly happy tourist stuff, but then the story of Israel, like the story of most countries, has its skeletons in the closet.

Up to Your Armpits in History

For those who are feeling especially macho, a visit to Hezekiah's water tunnel probably qualifies you for a gold Blue Peter badge, or the Israeli equivalent. The tunnel was cut in the time of the kings of Israel, around 700 years before Christ. The reason for it was that Jerusalem's one and only water supply at the time was a spring that bubbled up *outside* the walls of King Hezekiah's Jerusalem. Hezekiah was expecting a foreign invasion, and needed the water to be piped inside the walls as soon as possible. If not sooner.

So two teams of engineers started digging the tunnel from opposite ends – and amazingly they managed to meet in the middle by listening for the sounds of digging from each other. The water from the spring still flows down the tunnel, 2,700 years after it was cut – so the guys who built it certainly weren't cowboys. And they also managed to complete it on time. By the time the foreign troops had surrounded Jerusalem, the city had enough fresh water to outlast *any* siege.

The tunnel is 530 metres long, and most of the way it's only knee deep. The roof gets a bit low and the water drops to 1 metre deep in places, it's pitch black (you'll need a torch) *and* it's pretty cold down there. So if you don't enjoy the experience, you can't say that you weren't warned…

Hezekiah's water tunnel – cut 700 years before Christ.

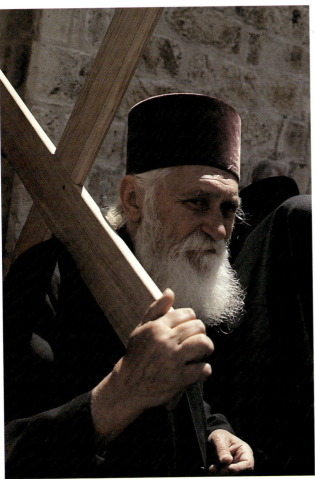

This man is part of the procession that travels the Via Dolorosa every Friday.

The *Via Dolorosa* is latin for the Street of Sorrows. This walk through Jerusalem marks (pretty inaccurately) the path Jesus followed from the place where he was condemned to the place where he was crucified. The path was first worked out in medieval times, and it's since become the holiest walk in Christianity – the way of the cross. Countless pilgrims follow it each year.

Along the Via Dolorosa are the 14 'stations' of the cross. Each station or stopping place marks a point on Jesus' journey as he carried his cross. The idea is that pilgrims can stop at each place and think about what the death of Jesus was all about.

Enter Pontius Pilate

Early on Good Friday morning, the Jewish Council had decided that Jesus should be put to death. It had to be done quickly because in just a few hours' time, at sunset, the Passover started, and they didn't want to be dealing with a crucified corpse over such a sacred festival.

The trouble was that only the Romans could put people to death. The Jewish authorities could write out the death warrant, but only Pontius Pilate, the Roman

Governor, could sign the thing. So as soon as it was light, Jesus was taken out of the cell where he had spent a wretched night, and was frog-marched across the city to the Roman fortress.

The first two stations on the Via Dolorosa cover what happened in this fortress. Here Pilate argued for a long time with the Jewish leaders about what should be done with Jesus. He knew that Jesus was innocent, but with the help of a crowd that was threatening to riot, they forced Pilate's hand.

At first he just had Jesus flogged, to see if that would satisfy them. Some prisoners died under a Roman flogging. Pilate then presented Jesus to the crowd so that they could see the condition he was in. But they *weren't* satisfied…

> *Pilate took Jesus outside and sat down on the judge's seat in the place called 'The Stone Pavement'. (In Hebrew the name is 'Gabbatha'.) It was then almost noon of the day before the Passover. Pilate said to the people, 'Here is your king!'*
>
> *They shouted back, 'Kill him! Kill him! Crucify him!'*
>
> *Pilate asked them, 'Do you want me to crucify your king?'*
>
> *The chief priests answered, 'The only king we have is the Emperor!'*
>
> *Then Pilate handed Jesus over to them to be crucified.*

A Game for the Soldiers

The Antonia Fortress, where all this happened, was a massive, square building, with a watchtower at each corner, and a pavement of hefty stone slabs in the central courtyard. It was on this pavement that Pontius Pilate sentenced Jesus.

The Stations of the Cross

1. Jesus condemned to death by Pilate
2. Jesus is given the cross
3. Jesus' first fall
4. Jesus and Mary his mother meet
5. Simon of Cyrene carries the cross
6. Veronica wipes Jesus' brow
7. Jesus' second fall
8. Jesus speaks to the women of Jerusalem
9. Jesus' third fall
10. Jesus is stripped
11. Jesus is crucified
12. Jesus dies
13. The body is taken from the cross
14. Jesus is buried in the tomb

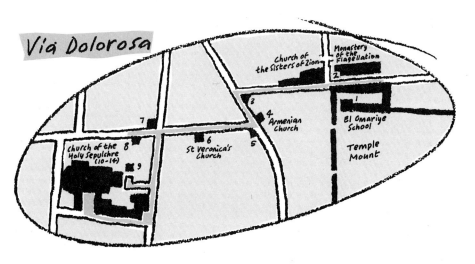

Via Dolorosa

Church of the Sisters of Zion

Monastery of the Flagellation 2

Armenian Church 4

El Omariye School 1

Church of the Holy Sepulchre (10-14) 8 9

St Veronica's Church 6

Temple Mount

3 7 5

Station 2 on the Via Dolorosa – the Chapel of the Flagellation. This is built on the site of the old Roman fortress where Jesus was flogged and condemned to death by Pontius Pilate.

The Antonia Fortress was demolished long ago. But the amazing thing is that parts of the pavement still exist. Demolition teams in ancient times were only interested in knocking down walls – ripping up the floor as well would be going a bit too far! Pilate's stone pavement can still be seen in the basement of the Convent of the Sisters of Zion.

Standing on these massive Roman stones sends a shudder up your spine. You're in the heart of the dreaded Antonia Fortress, and its ghost is all around you. 2,000 years ago this was the very last place you'd have wanted to be in Jerusalem. It was here, on *these* stones, that Jesus was whipped and sentenced. It was *this* pavement that heard the mob yelling for his blood.

The sisters of the convent do a brilliant guided tour, showing you the channels cut into the pavement that the Romans cut to collect the rainwater into massive cisterns below the fortress. The cisterns are still underground, and the channels still run into them.

There's one chilling little detail to complete the picture. Carved into several of the stones are the games the Roman soldiers used to play. The soldiers were pretty brutal, so we're not talking about cricket or hopscotch. One game, known as 'the King's Game' involved a condemned prisoner. We don't know the rules of the game any more, but a passage from one of the Gospels gives us the general idea…

Pilate's soldiers took Jesus into the governor's palace, and the whole company gathered round him. They stripped off his clothes and put a scarlet robe on him. Then they made a crown out of thorny branches and placed it on his head, and put a stick in his right hand. Then they knelt before him and mocked him. 'Long live the King of the Jews!' they said. They spat on him, and took the stick and hit him over the head. When they had finished mocking him, they took the robe off and put his own clothes back on him. Then they led him out to crucify him.

Roman soldiers' games scratched into the massive stones of the pavement.

Tour Guide Blues

Back out in the street you head west along the Via Dolorosa, following the same direction that Jesus took. In the summer, the street is very crowded and you have to push to make your way through. Every Friday there is a procession along the street, led by Franciscan monks, who carry a big wooden cross. It starts from Station 1 at 3 p.m., stopping at each station along the way.

If you're a visitor to Jerusalem, it's hard to get any peace and quiet on the Via Dolorosa. Arabs keep coming up to you, offering to give you a guided tour – and they won't take no for an answer. 'Let me show you the prison of Christ,' says one.

'Er, no thanks – nice of you to offer, though!'

'Then I will take you to the Dome of the Rock. Come, it is this way'.

'No – we wanted to go down here.'

'Ahhh! You are going to where the Christ died. I will show you.'

'No, *we're okay!*' Etc, etc, etc.

Even after you've practically shouted at them, you can end up by simply *falling into* one of their guided tours. It happens like this: as you walk along they walk beside you, telling you what is where, pointing out objects of interest, and generally wearing you down until you finally give in and let them show you round. Probably the best way to convince them that you aren't interested is to point at the most intelligent-looking member of your party (that's if *anyone* even roughly fits that description!) and say, 'He/She is our tour guide. We don't need two guides!'

This sometimes works, but these guys are profess-ionals and know the tourist trade inside out.

Some of these unofficial guides aren't too bad actually – and this *is* how they earn their living. The *official* guides wear badges and you can ferret them out at the Israeli tourist offices.

Eight Gates

One of the intriguing things about Jerusalem is that the Old City is surrounded by a wall. Various parts of the wall have walkways which give you a good view over the city. There are eight gates into the Old City some of which have interesting stories. Going clockwise around the city (and starting at 12 o'clock), here they are...

Damascus Gate was built by Suleiman the Magnificent between 1537 and 1540 (when the walls were being raised). It's a massive military gate, constructed for defence. On your way through, you have to go round a few corners, which was meant to slow down any would-be attackers. There is access from this gate onto the city wall.

Herod's Gate is so-called because it stands over the road that King Herod Antipas used to get away from it all at his palace.

Lion Gate has a wonderful legend attached to it. The story goes that Suleiman (the Magnificent one) had a bad dream one night. In it he was told to rebuild the walls around Jerusalem, or else be torn apart by lions. Suleiman went for the building option. He added the lions that appear over this gate in memory of his sleepless night. The gate is also known as Stephen's Gate, because Christian tradition has it that Stephen, the first Christian martyr, was led out of the city here to be stoned to death.

Golden Gate has been bricked up since 1530 and is surrounded by many stories and beliefs (see Chapter 4).

Dung Gate has its name because this is where the rubbish, etc, from the city was taken out to be chucked into the valley.

Zion Gate has a large number of bullet holes in it. These were made when Israeli troops tried to storm the Old City (held by the Jordanians) in 1948.

Jaffa Gate leads out onto the road to the Mediterranean coast and is the most important gate into the city. The gate itself stands to the left of the wide opening in the wall for traffic. This opening had to be made for the state visit of Kaiser Bill (the German Emperor) in 1898, who refused to get off his horse and walk into the city.

New Gate is very recent, dating from 1888. It's very boring, because it doesn't have any interesting legends attached to it!

Stations of the Cross

Each station along the Via Dolorosa is marked by a semi-circle of stones on the ground, and a number carved into the wall above it. Originally, there were only seven stations, and the 14 you can see now were finally decided upon in the last century.

Apparently, European pilgrims who had made the long journey to Israel were pretty fed up when they found there were only *seven* stations for them to visit. So due to demand, the other stations were specially created, even though no one had any real idea of where the events actually took place.

For this reason a walk along the Via Dolorosa is more a way of remembering Jesus' final walk than paying a visit to the actual places he passed. The streets he once walked in were demolished centuries ago, and are now part of the rubble 30 feet under the ground you walk on. As you follow the twists and turns of this walk, here are the stations you come to:

Station 3 is where Jesus is said to have fallen under the weight of the cross. Jesus wouldn't have been carrying the whole cross, just the horizontal piece, but this would be a massive load for anyone to carry. The Bible doesn't actually record that Jesus fell, but it's very likely he did, he was in such a weak condition.

Station 4 marks the place where it's believed Jesus passed Mary his mother. Again this event isn't in the Bible, but we know that Mary watched Jesus being crucified. When Jesus had just been born, an old prophet told Mary: 'Sorrow, like a sharp sword, will break your own heart'. If Mary *did* meet Jesus on the Via Dolorosa, then this is where that prophecy came true.

There's a very small chapel off the street here, with two very shabby grey doors. Above them is the engraving of a mother weeping over her son. Down in

The 4th Station of the cross on the Via Dolorosa. Here, Jesus is said to have met his mother as he carried the cross to the place of execution.

the church's ancient crypt there are two sandal-prints in a mosaic on the floor, to symbolise Mary standing, watching Jesus walk past to his death.

Station 5 was where the Roman guards forced a guy from Libya called Simon to carry the heavy crosspiece for Jesus…

> *On the way they met a man named Simon,*
> *who was coming into the city from the country,*
> *and the soldiers forced him to carry Jesus' cross.*

Jesus must have been in bad shape for the *soldiers* to take pity on him …

Station 6 was set up to mark a popular Catholic legend. According to the story, a woman called Veronica mopped Jesus' brow with a handkerchief as he walked past. After he had passed by, she was shocked to discover that his sweat had left a perfect image of his face on the cloth. Needless to say, the story isn't in the Bible's accounts of the crucifixion.

Station 7 is the point where Jesus is said to have stumbled and fallen for the second time. The Via Dolorosa now starts to climb uphill, step by step. And as Jesus must have done, you have to push your way through the crowds and the street-sellers to make any progress.

Station 8 brings us back to what actually happened, according to the Bible writers. Here Jesus stopped on the street...

> *A large crowd of people followed Jesus.*
> *Among them were some women who were*
> *weeping and wailing for him. Jesus turned to*
> *them and said, 'Women of Jerusalem! Don't cry*
> *for me, but for yourselves and your children. For*
> *the days are coming when people will say, 'How*
> *lucky are the women who never had children,*
> *who never bore babies, who never nursed them!'*

Jesus was talking about the total annihilation of Jerusalem, 40 years in the future, when the population was massacred.

Traders on the streets just outside the Church of the Holy Sepulchre.

Station 9 is the last station before you enter the Church of the Holy Sepulchre. The last five stations are inside the church itself. You reach the ninth station by going up a flight of stone steps on the right, off the street. It marks Jesus' third fall.

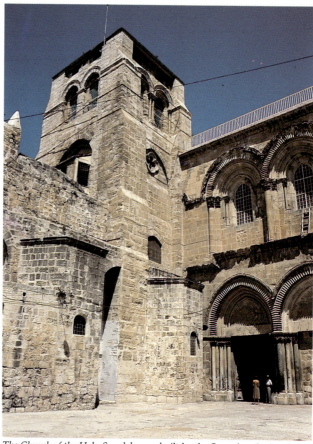

The Church of the Holy Sepulchre, as built by the Crusaders during the 1100s. The right-hand doorway was sealed up when the Muslims recaptured the Holy Land from the Crusaders.

Watching the Detectives

We're now about to enter the most remarkable church in the world. For viewers at home, here's the picture. Jesus was crucified on a small hill that was then *outside* Jerusalem's city walls. After he had died, he was laid to rest in a tomb at the foot of the hill. What has happened is that this church has been built *over the top* of the hill and the tomb, so that the most holy sites in Christianity are now *inside* the church. If that sounds strange, it's only because it *is* strange.

We have to thank our old friend St. Helena for the Church of the Holy Sepulchre. She was the one (if you remember) who plonked the Church of the Nativity over the cave in Bethlehem where Jesus was born. Helena had a real thing about finding sacred sites and putting churches over them. If you had a holy site, Helena had *just* the church to go with it. She was also wealthy enough to do all this, being the mother of the Roman Emperor, Constantine.

The big question is: How did they know that this was the right place? This is where we follow a bit of the detective work that Helena must have done. After the time of Jesus, the Christians living in Jerusalem grew rapidly in numbers. Even when Jerusalem was destroyed in AD 70, Christians carried on living here – and of course they knew *exactly* where Jesus had been executed and buried.

Then in AD 135, just when Jerusalem was getting back on its feet, the Emperor Hadrian (the one who built Hadrian's Wall, designed to keep the Scots out of England) came along and destroyed the city all over again. He decreed that any Jew who entered the city would be put to death. He also wanted to wipe out all traces of Christianity, so he covered the hill of the crucifixion and Jesus' tomb in concrete and built two pagan temples to the gods Jupiter and Venus over the top. It must have seemed like a smart move.

When Helena arrived here 200 years later, you didn't have to be the winner of *Mastermind* to spot the place where the crucifixion happened. With a massive lump of concrete and two temples, you couldn't miss it. Hadrian had hoped to bury Christianity in concrete, but instead he had brilliantly spotlighted the exact place he'd wanted to obliterate. This is technically known to archaeologists as 'cocking it up'.

Up the Hill to Death

Since Helena was here, the church has been altered and added to quite a lot. Walking around it is quite an experience. Unlike some of the other churches in the Holy Land, where natural lumps of rock come up through the floor, or there are caves in the basement, the really important bits in this church have been entirely hidden under layers of marble.

So if you walked in expecting to see the hill where Jesus died, you might be disappointed. The hill was long ago levelled off, cut into a neat cube-shape, fitted with a stone staircase and clothed from top to bottom in polished marble. You walk in through the main door and turn right up the steps to *Golgotha*, 'The Place

The altar on the site of the crucifixion in the Church of the Holy Sepulchre. Under the altar you can see the circular plate with a hole in its middle, where traditionally the cross is said to have rested in the earth.

of the Skull', where criminals in Jesus' day were put to death. At the top, 16 feet above floor level, are two chapels.

On the right is the Roman Catholic chapel. Stations 10 and 11, where Jesus was stripped and nailed to the cross, are in this chapel. On the left is the Greek Orthodox chapel. Traditionally, this is where the cross was raised with Jesus on it, and where he died. These are stations 12 and 13.

This is almost certainly the exact place where Jesus suffered and died. And if you can see beyond all the candles, statues, gold, bronze and marble, then the power of what took place here really hits you...

They took Jesus to a place called Golgotha, which means 'The Place of the Skull'. There they tried to give him wine mixed with a drug called myrrh, but Jesus would not drink it. Then they crucified him and divided his clothes among themselves, throwing dice to see who would get which piece of clothing.

It was nine o'clock in the morning when they crucified him. The notice of accusation against him said: 'The King of the Jews'. They also crucified two bandits with Jesus, one on his right and the other on his left.

People passing by shook their heads and hurled insults at Jesus. In the same way the chief priests and the teachers of the Law jeered at Jesus, saying to each other, 'He saved others, but he cannot save himself! Let us see the Messiah, the King of Israel, come down from the cross now, and we will believe in him!'

And the two who were crucified with Jesus insulted him also.

At noon the whole country was covered with darkness, which lasted for about three hours. At three o'clock Jesus cried out with a loud shout, 'Eloi, Eloi, lema sabachthani?' which means, 'My

God, my God, why did you abandon me?'
With a loud cry Jesus died.
The curtain hanging in the Temple was torn in two, from top to bottom. The army officer who was standing there in front of the cross saw how Jesus had died. 'This man was really the Son of God!' he said.

With the Pilgrims

It's in the Greek Orthodox chapel that the pilgrims gather, standing back respectfully from the altar. This chapel is really very ornate. It has a quite small altar that is box-shaped. On it are two enormous candle-sticks in the shape of palm trees, and behind them, dominating the scene, is a large cross with a metal cut-out of Christ on it.

The focus for the pilgrims' devotion lies underneath the altar. It's amazing to think that for many of the people here, coming to Golgotha is a lifetime's ambition. And yet the force of the crowds means that you only have a few seconds to spend underneath this cross.

What happens is this. When it's your turn, you stoop down and kneel right under the altar. Right inside there is a circular brass plate, showing the different stages of the cross on it. In the very middle of the plate is a large hole, where you put your hand. This is meant to be the actual place where the cross was dropped into the earth.

I have to say that it's really not to my taste – it's far too ornate and in a way too precious. But the fact that so many millions of pilgrims think of this as one of the holiest places in the world gives it a unique atmosphere.

Coming down the steps from the hill of the crucifixion, there is a flat, pinkish stone lying opposite the main door to the church. Under the pink stone is a rock where Jesus is said to have been annointed with special spices before being buried. The rock underneath had to be covered because people kept breaking bits off and taking them home with them – a sort of holy vandalism!

If you want to see the only bit of Golgotha left that hasn't been built on, you can go into the Chapel of Adam, where the naked rock face is protected behind a glass screen.

Uniquely Eccentric

The Church of the Holy Sepulchre is really quite outrageous. Every square inch of the building is encrusted – with paintings, a forest of candles, great golden lamps hanging like bats from the ceilings, thick marble columns, statues of assorted saints, heavily-draped altars and thick, weird carvings around the little doorways. And as you wander round, bewildered at it all, you almost get flattened by priests in flapping black robes, speeding from chapel to chapel, closely followed by billowing clouds of sickly incense. This church would easily walk away with the Liberace Award for Subtlety.

So why have they done it? One way of thinking of it is like this. In the West, to preserve a special place, we try to keep it exactly as it was, so that people can imagine what it must have been like long ago. But this church isn't a Western church. In the East, the best way to honour this holy site was to 'glorify' it with gold, silver, precious stones and all the rest. It was their way of saying how special this place is. Their way of expressing their appreciation for what Jesus Christ did here.

However, the Church of the Holy Sepulchre can also be a pretty fierce place. Six Christian denominations live in the church in a state of permanent Cold War. In descending order of territory, there are the

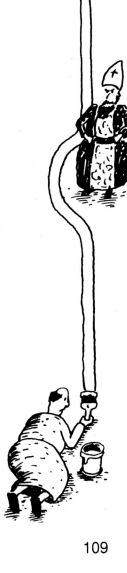

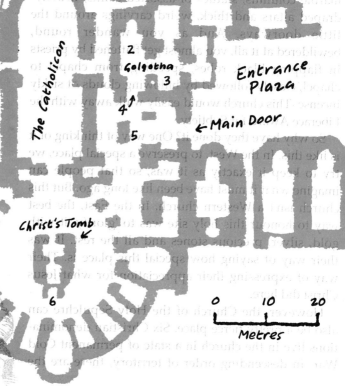

Church of the Holy Sepulchre

Crypt of St Helena

1 Crypt of the Finding of the Cross
2 Greek Calvary Chapel
3 Catholic Calvary Chapel
4 Chapel of Adam
5 Stone of Anointing
6 Copts' Chapel

The Catholicon

Golgotha

Entrance Plaza

← Main Door

Christ's Tomb

0   10   20
Metres

Believe it Or Not...

The Church of the Holy Sepulchre plays host to two of the most strange ceremonies in the history of Christianity. Both are carried out on Easter Saturday, on the night before Christ rose from the dead. They date from ancient times.

The Ceremony of the Holy Fire is performed by the Greek and Armenian patriarchs. Crowds of people crush around the tomb in the middle of the church, while the two patriarchs are led into the tomb. The atmosphere is like a football match, with the crowd shrieking , singing and shoving. The tomb is sealed. Suddenly the patriarchs push two flaming torches through two openings in the tomb's wall. The crowd goes bananas, lighting their candles from the fire that many believe has been 'sent from God'.

Searching for the Body of Christ is a much more sober affair. The Ethiopian monks who live on the church's rooftop spend the early hours of Easter Sunday morning in a ceremonial search for Jesus' body. By doing this, they act out the initial confusion of Jesus' disciples when they discovered that his tomb was empty.

Greek Orthodox, Roman Catholics, Armenians, Syrians, Copts (from Egypt) and Abyssinians (from Ethiopia). The Abyssinians are the unluckiest of the lot. They used to own a lot of territory in medieval times, but since then they've been forced out of the church to live up on the roof under the blistering sun in tiny little cells. All the squabbles make the church a colourful (and sometimes hostile) place.

At the heart of the Church of the Holy Sepulchre is the sepulchre itself – the tomb where Jesus is said to have been laid. The story of Jesus' tomb deserves a special chapter, so this is where Chapter 6 ends...

7 AT THE EMPTY TOMB

In the middle of the Church of the Holy Sepulchre, right underneath a great dome, is the structure that gives this church its name – the tomb of Christ. This is the 14th Station of the cross, marking Jesus' burial. The great symbol of the Christian faith is, of course, the cross. But an equally good symbol to sum up Christianity would be an empty grave. Because it was here, 2,000 years ago, that some very strange events happened...

A Borrowed Grave

After Jesus died, a rich friend of his, Joseph of Arimathea, asked Pilate for his body. He wanted to give his friend a decent burial. Pilate agreed. So Joseph took the body down from the cross, wrapped it in linen, and prepared Jesus in traditional Jewish fashion for burial. He then placed Jesus' body in a new tomb, dug out of rock in a garden right next to Golgotha. Joseph had been keeping the tomb for when he'd need it himself. The tomb had a heavy stone disk which was rolled across the entrance to seal it.

A stone like this one (which is in the Garden Tomb) was used to seal the entrance of Jesus' tomb. It was discovered rolled aside on the morning when his body went missing.

If it's true that Joseph's tomb is now enshrined in the middle of the Church of the Holy Sepulchre, then he'd have difficulty in recognising it now! For a start, it's no longer a cave. Apparently, the original builders of the church dug all around the tomb, leaving it standing on its own on a flat floor – as it appears today. It's also been given the Eastern 'treatment': loads of carvings, lamps, marble slabs and all the rest.

You pass under an ornate, low doorway to get inside. The first room feels small enough, but when you've passed through an even lower doorway into the tomb itself, it feels really quite claustrophobic. If more than four of you go in together, you have to take it in turns to breathe. A small priest wearing black robes and a black hat stands in this room. On your

The Hill of the Skull, with its strange, skull-like eye sockets. Many Christians believe that this is the place where Jesus was crucified.

right is a great marble slab with flowers, candles and lamps on and around it. According to tradition, this is where Jesus was finally placed.

Around the back of the tomb is a minute little chapel – in fact, it's more like a kiosk! This chapel belongs to the Egyptian Copts (one of the oldest branches of Christianity). This tiny space is the only bit of the church they own. If you go inside, the priest will show you, under a curtain at floor level, a small space where the Copts say Christ's head lay. But beware! In this space are some large-denomination shekel bills, placed there as a none-too-subtle hint. Perhaps the gifts pay the rent on the chapel...

The Alternative Tomb

If you don't like the Church of the Holy Sepulchre generally, then the tomb will probably be the last straw! But fortunately, there is an alternative site for the death and burial of Christ. This is in a place called 'The Garden Tomb' and is just outside the Damascus Gate on the north side of the city.

As the story goes, the British General, Gordon of Khartoum, was staying in Jerusalem on leave in 1883. He was quite a religious chap, but he wasn't a great fan of the Church of the Holy Sepulchre, which in those days was even more of a riot than it is now. Gordon was sure that the place where Jesus died and was buried must be outside the present walls of Jerusalem.

One evening, as he was looking out of his hotel window near the Damascus Gate, Gordon saw a rocky hill which looked uncannily like a skull, just beyond the walls. Jesus had been crucified, according to the Bible, outside the city walls at a place called 'The Skull'. Before this, everyone had thought the place was called 'The Skull' because it was a much-used execution ground. But what if the place actually *looked* like a skull as well?

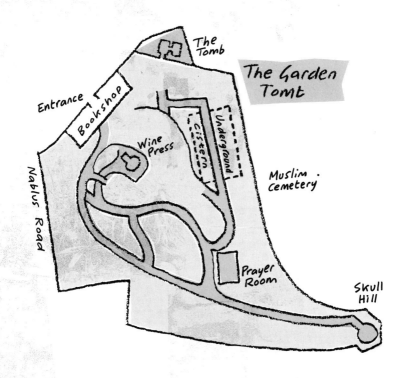

The Garden Tomb

To complete the puzzle, a small tomb from the time of Jesus was found at the foot of the hill – which exactly matched the Bible's description of Jesus' tomb. Skull Hill now overlooks a noisy, dirty Arab bus station, while nearby the tomb is in a beautifully peaceful garden owned by Christians.

Visiting the tomb is intriguing – it looks and feels authentic, like something straight out of the Bible (which of course is just what's claimed for it). There is even a large groove in the rock floor outside the entrance, where the massive stone disk to seal the tomb would have been rolled.

After squeezing through the narrow doorway, you find yourself in the first of two small rooms tunnelled

The Garden Tomb was discovered by two Greek brothers digging here at the end of the last century. It is definitely a tomb from the time of Jesus – but is it _the_ tomb?

out of the rock. Looking into the second room, there are two burial places carved out. The whole place is very well made, and must have belonged originally to a rich family. Was this the family tomb of Joseph of Arimathea?

When you think about it, the Garden Tomb has

'Very early on Sunday morning, the women went to the tomb, carrying the spices they had prepared. They found the stone rolled away from the entrance to the tomb...'

exactly the same pattern as the Church of the Holy Sepulchre: a hill with a two-roomed tomb right next to it.

Early One Sunday Morning

The great thing about the Garden Tomb (whether this is the actual place or not) is that it's unspoilt and out in the open air, away from all those lamps, candles and statues. The Hill of the Skull looks eerie and nasty enough to be a killing ground, and stepping into the tomb helps you to understand what happened all those years ago. It was on the Sunday after Jesus died...

Early on Sunday morning, while it was still dark, Mary Magdalen went to the tomb and saw that the stone had been taken away from the entrance. She went running to Simon Peter and the other disciple, whom Jesus loved, and told them, 'They have taken the Lord from the tomb, and we don't know where they have put him...'

Mary stood crying outside the tomb. While she was still crying, she bent over and looked in the tomb and saw two angels there dressed in white, sitting where the body of Jesus had been, one at the head and the other at the feet. 'Woman, why are you crying?' they asked her.

She answered, 'They have taken my Lord away, and I do not know where they have put him!'

Then she turned round and saw Jesus standing there; but she did not know that it was Jesus. 'Woman , why are you crying?', Jesus asked her. 'Who is it that you are looking for?'

She thought he was the gardener, so she said to him, 'If you took him away, sir, tell me where you have put him, and I will go and get him.'

Jesus said to her, 'Mary!'

She turned towards him and said in Hebrew, 'Rabboni' (This means 'Teacher'.)

This was just the first of many meetings between the risen Jesus and his followers, according to the Bible's writers. At first they refused to believe that Jesus had come back from the dead. But then, after seeing him for themselves, they were completely convinced – and they were overjoyed. It changed their lives for ever. This was the start of the Christian faith.

Mix-ups

Lots of people say that the resurrection simply *couldn't* have happened. Dead people don't get up and walk, especially after a gruesome death like Jesus'. There must be something wrong with the stories told

Inside the Garden Tomb – where the body would have been placed.

in the Bible. There must be another explanation for what *really* took place. Here are some alternatives to the resurrection. They fall into two groups – that a simple mistake was made, or that there was some trickery afoot.

The first 'mistake' explanation is that Jesus wasn't crucified. In the crowded streets along the Via Dolorosa, Jesus was mixed up with an innocent bystander. The soldiers took *him*, instead of Jesus. Simon of Cyrene, who helped carry Jesus' cross, is the favourite in this switch of prisoners. Jesus escaped and came out of hiding after a few days, pretending that he'd risen from the grave.

This theory is neat, but it's a bit hard to swallow. It's hard to believe that the Roman execution squad would be that careless, or that stupid. They were professional soldiers, and mistakes like that were paid for severely.

Another explanation is that Jesus didn't really die on the cross. He passed out in the pain and was carried down in a sort of coma. Everyone – even the soldiers who had seen *real* death a thousand times before – mistook him for dead. In the cool of the tomb he woke up, escaped, and appeared to his followers as the conqueror of death.

It's a nice idea, but the injuries that Jesus received on that Friday would put him on any hospital's critical list for a long, long time. Rolling heavy stones from tomb entrances and walking even short distances on lacerated feet would have been just impossible.

Foul Play?

So if there weren't any mistakes, was there some trickery at work on the first Easter Sunday morning? Perhaps the disciples came along at dead of night and whisked away Jesus' body. They then pointed to the empty tomb and said that Jesus had risen.

The big question here is: *why do it?* It's clear from the Bible that the disciples were totally shattered by Jesus' death – they hadn't expected it, and they were scared stiff that the Romans were coming to get them as well. They were more interested in hiding away behind locked doors than starting up a new religion. There they hid, in the locked and bolted Upper Room, terrified that there would be a fatal knock on the door in the dead of the night...

And then suddenly everything seemed to change. The disciples were transformed by something, so that they started to preach on the street corners about Jesus being alive again. On Good Friday, Peter swore that he'd never even heard of Jesus, he was so terrified. But after Easter Sunday, nothing could stop him from telling crowds of people about Jesus. Over the years, most of the disciples were executed for refusing to keep quiet about Jesus' death and resurrection. What changed them? There's nothing that can really explain their change better than that they met Jesus, alive after his death.

Another theory is that the Jewish authorities tricked the disciples by removing the body themselves. They did it to pre-empt the disciples from doing the same. If this is true, then why didn't they simply produce Jesus' dead body when all the fuss about the resurrection started?

Of course, there's no concrete *proof* that Jesus rose from the dead. But there's enough evidence to show that you can believe in the resurrection without having to kiss your brain goodbye.

Back to Galilee

Well, we've now reached the end of our pilgrimage. Probably the best place to come at the end of the journey is the little church of Peter's Primacy by the

The church at Tabgha in Galilee, built on the rock where Jesus is said to have met his disciples after he was raised from the dead.

Sea of Galilee at Tabgha. You were promised earlier in the book that we'd come back to this peaceful place. It's also appropriate to end the book with a breakfast scene (from the Bible), as it started off with breakfast after landing in Israel.

The reason to be here is that it was somewhere along this lake shore that Jesus appeared to a few of his disciples as they were out fishing. This church was built to celebrate the meeting which took place (like many events in the Bible) early in the morning...

> Simon Peter said to the other disciples, 'I am going fishing.'
> 'We will come with you,' they told him. So they went out in a boat, but all that night they did not catch a thing. As the sun was rising, Jesus stood at the water's edge, but the disciples did not know that it was Jesus. Then he asked them, 'Young men, haven't you caught anything?'
> 'Not a thing,' they answered.
> He said to them, 'Throw your net out on the right side of the boat, and you will catch some. So they threw the net out and could not pull it back in, because they had caught so many fish.
> The disciple whom Jesus loved said to Peter, 'It is the Lord!' When Peter heard that it was the Lord, he wrapped his outer garment round him (for he had taken his clothes off) and jumped into the water. The other disciples came to shore in the boat, pulling the net full of fish. They were not very far from land, about 100 metres away. When they stepped ashore, they saw a charcoal fire there with fish on it and some bread.
> Then Jesus said to them, 'Bring some of the fish you have just caught.'

The rock in the middle of this church has been accepted for centuries as the place where Jesus cooked his disciples this breakfast. It sounds incredible. The

Jerusalem Info

If you're visiting Jerusalem, it's worth paying a visit on your first day to an Israel Government Tourist Office. There's one just inside the Jaffa Gate, on the left.

The office will be able to give you an assortment of leaflets that detail different (and *reliable*) walking tours around the city. It also has a selection of Jerusalem's newsheets and magazines, telling you what's on where.

Don't pick all these up on your last day – you'll only kick yourself when you get home!

risen Jesus wasn't doing what you might expect – floating two feet off the ground like some heavenly visitor. Instead he was rolling his sleeves up, getting his hands dirty lighting fires, and *cooking breakfast!* He was as real as bacon and eggs – it wasn't a ghost they were seeing!

Coming to the Holy Land as a pilgrim (rather than just as a tourist) is really about that – discovering the reality that lies beneath all the holy sites, religious souvenirs and the busy streets. Finding the real, risen Jesus is the best thing anyone could bring away from a visit to these special places, or from reading about them in a book like this. As Jesus once put it, 'Ask, and you will receive. Seek, and you will find. Knock, and the door will be opened to you.'

APPENDICES

APPENDIX A

Who Was Who?

This list is made up of a very mixed bunch – sinners and saints, rebels, vindictive rulers, heroes and great leaders. They've all played a part in the shaping of the Holy Land as it is today...

Abraham The Father of Israel. All Jews trace their descent back to him. Lived around 1900 BC, had great faith in God. His burial cave is near Hebron.

Absalom Rebellious son of King David. Led a revolt against his father and died after getting his head caught in the branches of a tree. See Tomb of Absalom, Jerusalem.

Ahab Vicious Old Testament king, led Israel into worship of false gods. See Megiddo.

Andrew One of Jesus' 12 disciples, brother to Simon Peter.

Bar Cochba, Simon Led a revolt against Roman rule in AD 132. His rebels captured Jerusalem and built a Temple. Rebellion brutally crushed by Emperor Hadrian, three years later.

Begin, Manachem Leader of the Irgun, an Israeli terrorist group which blew up Jerusalem's King David hotel in 1946. Begin was later Prime Minister of Israel.

Ben Gurion, David First Prime Minister of the modern

state of Israel. On 14 May 1948 Ben Gurion proclaimed Israel to be an independent state.

Caiaphas High Priest at the time of Jesus. He pronounced the Jewish death sentence upon Jesus. See Caiaphas' House, Mt Zion.

Constantine First Christian Emperor, converted in AD 313. Under his rule, many Christian sites were found in the Holy Land.

David King of Israel around 1000 BC. David was also a great writer of psalms and defeater of the giant Goliath. He was later seen as Israel's ideal king.

Dayan, Moshe Israeli military hero, especially during the 1948 and 1956 wars.

Eleazer Leader of the Jewish rebels who occupied Masada against the Romans. Eleazer's speech convinced the rebels to commit mass suicide rather than surrender. See Masada.

Elijah Fierce prophet at the time of King Ahab. On Mt Carmel he had 450 prophets of the false God Baal put to death.

Hadrian Roman Emperor. In AD 135, he flattened Jerusalem and built a Roman city on top of the ruins, giving it the catchy name 'Aelia Capitolina'. He also desecrated the sites of the crucifixion and resurrection by building pagan temples over them. Remains of Aelia Capitolina can still be seen (some are in the Jewish Quarter).

Helena, St Former barmaid in Bithynia, later mother of Roman Emperor Constantine. In the 4th century

AD she visited Israel and unearthed many Christian holy sites – only to cover them again with churches. See Church of the Nativity (Bethlehem), Church of the Holy Sepulchre (Jerusalem).

Herod Antipas Son of Herod the Great. He had John the Baptist beheaded and interrogated Jesus before the crucifixion.

Herod the Great Puppet King of Judea when Jesus was born. Herod was the builder of the Temple that Jesus saw (see Wailing Wall, and the Herodian, near Bethlehem).

Herzl, Theodor Born a Hungarian Jew, Herzl was the founder of Zionism (the call for a political state of Israel) which began in the 1890s. See the Herzl Museum, Jerusalem.

Jacob Grandson of Abraham. The descendants of his 12 sons eventually became the 12 tribes of Israel.

James One of Jesus' 12 disciples. James, Peter and John were the three closest to Jesus.

Jesus Christ Carpenter from Nazareth, leader of the 12 disciples, teacher, healer and miracle-worker. Crucified during the rule of Pontius Pilate. Reported alive again three days later. The founder and focus of the Christian faith.

Jezebel Wicked Queen of King Ahab, had various people put to death.

John One of Jesus' 12 disciples. John, James and Peter were the three closest to Jesus.

John the Baptist Prophet who preached and baptised by the River Jordan just before Jesus started his work. See Jericho.

Joseph Carpenter in Nazareth, husband to Mary, the mother of Jesus.

Joseph Old Testament character (the son of Jacob) who was sold by his brothers to slave-traders. Joseph ended up as Prime Minister of Egypt during a famine, and thus saved his family (brothers and all) from starvation.

Joseph of Arimathea Made room in the tomb he had built for himself to take the body of Jesus. See Church of the Holy Sepulchre, Garden Tomb.

Joshua Military leader of Israel after Moses, when the nation was trying to conquer the Promised Land. See Jericho.

Judas Iscariot The 13th member of Jesus' group, who betrayed Jesus to his enemies and then committed suicide.

Luke Early follower of Jesus who wrote an account of his life, *Luke's Gospel*.

Maccabeus, Judas Leader of a successful revolt against Seleucid (Syrian) rule in 165 BC. Judas and his four brothers captured Jerusalem's Temple Mount and restored it as the focus of the Jewish faith.

Mark Writer of *Mark's Gospel*. Mark probably owned the Upper Room, where Jesus and his disciples ate the Last Supper. See Coenaculum, Jerusalem.

Mary Mother of Jesus, venerated today by millions of Catholics and Orthodox Christians. See Nazareth, Via Dolorosa.

Mary Magdalene Prostitute who became a follower of Jesus. Mary was one of the first people to see Jesus alive again after he was crucified.

Matthew One of Jesus' 12 disciples. Possibly the writer of *Matthew's Gospel*.

Moses First great leader of Israel. Moses led the nation out of slavery in Egypt to become a free people. On Mt Sinai (in the Sinai Desert), he received the 10 Commandments and the Jewish Law from God. The *Law of Moses* (the first five books of the Bible) are at the heart of the Jewish faith.

Nehemiah Rebuilder of Jerusalem after the Jewish people returned from a seventy-year exile in Babylon, about 450 BC.

Paul Persecutor of the first Christians, Paul was converted and became the great communicator of the Christian faith throughout the Roman Empire.

Peter One of Jesus' 12 disciples. Peter, James and John were the three closest to Jesus. See Peter's House, Capernaum.

Pontius Pilate Procurator of the Roman province of Judea from AD 26. Pilate's rule in Israel was harsh and repressive. Sometime around AD 30 he had Jesus Christ condemned to death. See Gabbatha.

Saladin Powerful Muslim leader who defeated the Crusaders and took Jerusalem in 1187.

Samson A colourful, wild-west character who led Israel before the nation had proper kings. Samson had amazing powers of strength, which he used on Israel's enemies, the Philistines.

Samuel The last of Israel's 'judges'. Samuel anointed Saul as Israel's first king.

Saul As first king of Israel, Saul was a disaster. He ended up by falling in battle to the Philistines on Mt Gilboa.

Solomon Son of King David. Solomon's rule was a kind of golden age for Israel. He and the royal court lived in the height of luxury, Solomon had 700 wives (plus 300 mistresses), and he was renowned for his pearls of wisdom. Friend of the famous Queen of Sheba (who still makes appearances on sherry adverts!) See Megiddo.

Stephen The first Christian martyr. In the early months of Christianity, after Jesus had ascended, Stephen was stoned to death outside the city walls for preaching about Jesus. See the Lion Gate, Jerusalem (also called Stephen's Gate).

Suleiman the Magnificent Ottoman sultan, ruler of the Turkish Empire. Under him, Jerusalem was given a new lease of life – new walls and gates (which still stand), drinking fountains (some of which still work), new markets, etc.

Thomas One of Jesus' disciples. He doubted at first that Jesus had risen from death, but was convinced when Jesus appeared to him. For this reason he is still known as 'Doubting Thomas'.

Titus Son the the Roman Emperor Vespasian. In AD 70, he was sent to regain control of Jerusalem after a revolt by the Jews against the Roman rule. His siege of the city ended in disaster as the Romans demolished it, along with the Temple, and massacred the population.

Weizmann, Chaim Second leader of the Zionist movement. He strongly influenced the British after 1917 in securing a homeland for the Jewish people.

APPENDIX B

Recorded Highlights of Holy Land History

The story of the Holy Land spans over 3,000 years. A lot can happen in that much time. So it's not surprising to find that you can occasionally/often/usually (delete where applicable) get lost in all the details. This lightning history of Israel gives a rapid rundown of what *roughly* happened when, where, and to who...

The Runaway Slaves

The Jewish people trace their descent back to Abraham, living some time after 2000 BC. While travelling through Palestine (then called Canaan) he was promised this land by God for his descendants to call their own.

But some 800 years later, Abraham's descendants were far from being an independent nation. Instead they were a group of cruelly-treated slaves in Egypt. Then, according to the Bible, God called a young Jew, Moses, to lead the people out to freedom in 'the Promised Land'.

With many miraculous interventions from God, Moses brought the people out from slavery to Mt Sinai. Here God appeared to Moses and gave him the Jewish Law (including the 10 Commandments). The people of Israel became *God's* people, bound to him by a solemn agreement. This event marked the beginning of the Jewish faith.

Israelites Move In

In approx 1230 BC, the young nation of Israel, led by Joshua (Moses' successor), took the Holy Land by storm. Because of God's promise to Abraham, they believed that their invasion was by divine command. They managed to conquer most of the different peoples living there. It was during this conquest that the walls of Jericho collapsed at the sound of Israeli trumpet blasts.

The Judges

For the next 250 years, Israel was ruled by a series of 'judges' (they were actually military leaders). Life was rough then as Israel's partially-defeated enemies waged guerilla warfare in revenge. The judges themselves included some colourful, maverick characters, like Samson (addicted to practical jokes and beautiful women), Gideon (who used bizarre battle techniques) and Deborah (the wild woman judge).

Give Us a King!

The people grew tired of the unpredictable judges and demanded a king to rule them and to (hopefully) finish off their enemies. They were given the crazed King Saul, who ruled badly. Following him came King David, who began his reign around 1010 BC. David started by capturing Jerusalem and making it his capital. This marked the beginning of a turbulent 3,000 year history for the city.

David and his son Solomon were a great success for Israel politically. They stopped the guerilla wars and expanded Israel's territory. David was famous for his songwriting (he wrote many psalms that are in the Bible), his giantkilling (polishing off Goliath with a stone) and his affair with Bathsheba (one of his soldiers' wives). Solomon was famous for his multiple marriages, his fabulous wealth and wisdom. Solomon built the First Temple in Jerusalem.

A Divided Land

But after Solomon, disaster struck the nation. The north rebelled against the south and the kingdom split in two. There were now two kings – one ruling Israel (the north), the other ruling Judah (the south). The split occurred around 930 BC. The two nations lived uneasily with each other and the division was never healed. Around this time came the prophets. These were men who brought God's message to both nations. They included Elijah, Jeremiah, Isaiah, Amos, Hosea, and many more. In a nutshell, they told the people that they had rebelled against God, and unless there were some radical changes then God's punishment would soon follow.

In Chains

And God's punishment *did* follow, just as predicted. In 722 BC Israel was smashed by the troops of the mighty Assyrian Empire. Its people were led off into exile, never to return. The same happened to Judah 136 years later (in 586 BC). They were carted off to exile by King Nebuchadnezzar in Bablyon, leaving behind the smoking ruins of Jerusalem. It looked as though the Jewish people were completely washed up.

Return from Exile

Then the Babylonian Empire (which kept the Jews in exile) was defeated by King Cyrus of Persia. Cyrus was a quite humane ruler and allowed the exiles to return home and rebuild Jerusalem. The Temple was rebuilt under the rule of Zerubbabel, the appointed governor, around the year 515 BC. This is known as 'the Second Temple' (King Solomon's being the first). Another group, led by Nehemiah (former wine-taster to the Emperor), settled in the city and reconstructed Jerusalem's walls. The story up to this point is recorded in the Old Testament of the Bible.

Plaything of the Superpowers

The story of the land between the Old and New Testaments shows the Jewish people at the mercy of the great powers of the time. They never regained the full independence as a nation that they had enjoyed under the kings.

In 332 BC, Jerusalem surrendered to the Greek military whizz-kid Alexander the Great and was absorbed into the Greek Empire. Many gallons of bloodshed later, in 198 BC, Palestine fell into the hands of the Seleucids – the Greek–Syrian Empire.

The mad ruler Antiochus Epiphanes came to the throne in 175 BC. He insisted that everyone in his empire should adopt Greek culture, and he waged a terrorisation campaign against those who held out against this (including the Jews). In 169 BC the Jerusalem Temple was ransacked and a statue of the god Zeus set up inside – the ultimate desecration for the Jews. The Jewish religion was effectively abolished.

Jewish Rebellion

The Jewish High Priest and his five sons plotted a revolt, which was led by one of the sons, Judas Maccabeus. After a bloody three-year guerilla war the Temple was cleaned up and the Jewish faith made safe from Antiochus.

Eventually Simon (the youngest of the five brothers) became the High Priest and ruler of the semi-independent Palestine. Over the next 120 years, Simon's descendants 'governed' the nation. It was a period of intrigues, plots, bitter arguments and murder among the ruling family members.

The Romans are Coming!

In 63 BC the Romans stepped in and ended the arguments. General Pompey took Jerusalem, damaging the 450 year-old Temple, and killing large numbers of the inhabitants. Judea (as Palestine was now called) became a small province of the Roman Empire, with a reputation for trouble. Being sent to govern *Judea* was like being sent to a political graveyard!

In 40 BC Herod was sent from Rome to do just that, and he was given the title 'King of the Jews'. Herod was only a remote-controlled king (the real power was still in Rome), but he was a powerful character in his own right.

The Herod Years

King Herod was a man with big ideas. He rebuilt large sections of Jerusalem, including posh Roman buildings such as an amphitheatre. He built his luxury hideaway palace on top of Masada, by the Dead Sea. But his greatest building work was to completely reconstruct Zerubbabel's old Temple, starting around 20 BC. The Temple was finished long after his death.

Around the year 4 BC, a son was born to a Galilean peasant couple. They called him Jesus. In AD 27 he began his public works, which included preaching, healing, and wonder-working. Around the year AD 30, he was put to death by crucifixion under the order of the Roman Procurator Pontius Pilate. He was reported alive again three days later by his followers. This marked the beginning of the Christian faith.

The Jerusalem Disaster

Anti-Roman terrorist attacks increased in Judea soon after the time of Jesus. The Zealots (a Jewish terrorist network) finally led the nation into an uprising in AD 66. The Romans gave their standard, none-too-subtle response: they sent in the troops who brutally wiped out the troublemakers.

In AD 70, after a short siege by the Roman General Titus, Jerusalem received its usual treatment in situations like these: all its major buildings were flattened, the Temple destroyed for ever, the population massacred. Three years later, the final Zealot stronghold on Masada was crushed.

Almost exactly the same thing happened in AD 135. The Emperor Hadrian decided to rebuild Jerusalem as a pagan Roman city, calling it Aelina Capitolina. This led to a fresh Jewish revolt, resulting in the predictable destruction of Jerusalem. Aelia Capitolina was built on the still-warm ruins, with temples to Jupiter and Venus covering the sites where Jesus was believed to have died and risen.

The Search for Holy Sites

In AD 313 the Roman Emperor Constantine was converted to Christianity. The empire took the Christian faith as its 'official' religion. Constantine sent his mother on a special mission to the Holy Land to seek out the holy sites. She built churches in various places, including the Churches of the Nativity and the Holy Sepulchre in Bethlehem and Jerusalem. Jerusalem became a Christian city, and Jews were forbidden to enter it.

In AD 395 the Roman Empire divided into Eastern and Western halves. The Eastern Empire was ruled from Byzantium (renamed Constantinople, and now called Istanbul). Byzantium gave its name to the new empire: the Byzantine Empire. Palestine was a province of this empire for some 350 years. In later years Jewish people were persecuted, and some were forcibly 'converted'.

The Tide of Islam

Just to complicate matters, a *third* religion now

trained its sights on Palestine. Around the year AD 610, a man living in the Arabian city of Mecca called Muhammed believed that he had started to receive messages from God. These messages were later written down to form the Qur'an (or Koran). Muhammed's followers quickly grew, despite opposition, and Islam began to spread rapidly as a religious and political force.

One day in AD 638, Caliph Omar plus his desert troops knocked on Jerusalem's gates and was allowed in. Their achievement was a unique record in Jerusalem's history: the city had been captured without a drop of blood being spilt! The Temple Mount was declared an Islamic holy site, and work began on building the mosques which still stand on it. Jews and Christians were allowed to live and worship in peace.

The city was in Islamic hands for the next four centuries – until acts of cruelty against Christian pilgrims provoked the first of the Crusades.

Holy War!

The Crusades were a series of 'holy' wars, launched by the Pope, in an effort to reclaim the Holy Land for Christianity. In 1099 the Crusaders (drawn from many European countries) conquered Jerusalem and brutally butchered the Jews and Muslims living there. Palestine was christened 'the Latin Kingdom of Jerusalem'. The Dome of the Rock was converted into a Christian church, and the Church of the Holy Sepulchre was rebuilt – its exterior looking pretty much as it does today.

However, only 88 years later there was another 'holy' war, and this time God seemed to be on the other side. The Muslim army, led by the much-feared Saladin, defeated the Crusaders and drove them out.

Breathing Space

From 1260, Palestine entered a reasonably peaceful chapter of its history, ruled by the Mamelukes. They were Egyptian Islamic rulers. Their sultan (with the unlikely name of Babybars) demolished Jerusalem's few remaining walls and did a lot of new building work. Jerusalem became a centre of Islamic learning.

Turkish Takeover

Palestine now began a new era that only ended in the 20th century. In 1517, the country was overrun by the Turkish Ottoman Empire. Sultan Suleiman the Magnificent came to power shortly afterwards and set about major rebuilding in Jerusalem. He installed the walls and gates which can still be seen around the Old City. The empire was Muslim, so there was no change in religion, and the Ottomans continued to tolerate Christianity in Palestine.

However, the Turkish Empire was suffering a slow death, and gradually Palestine became a forgotten, decaying corner of the empire. Jerusalem deteriorated into a dog-eared city. In the late 19th century, the Jewish people, long exiled from Palestine, started to come home. The waves of immigration were small at first, but increased with the arrival of the new century.

In the 1890s, the Zionist movement was born, which had as its central aim the restoration of the lands of the Bible (known as *Eretz* Israel) to the Jewish people.

Land of Hope and Glory

Then in 1917 the sleepy Turkish Empire finally fell asleep for good. The British General Allenby entered Jerusalem through the Jaffa Gate and the country came under British administration. Between 1917 and 1948 Palestine was under the 'British Mandate' (recognised by the League of Nations). Their aim was to create a homeland for the Jewish people, but without restricting the rights of the Arab people who had lived in Palestine for centuries (the Palestinians).

This aim led to a great deal of anti-Jewish rioting throughout the country. Understandably, the Palestinians were not too keen to move over and make room for a new state on the territory they knew as *their* home. On the Jewish side, they claimed the land as theirs because they had lived there in biblical times and because Jews had continued (in small numbers) to live there ever since.

As the arguments and the violence boiled over, the British started to backtrack, restricting Jewish immigration into Palestine. This in turn led to terrorist attacks by underground Israeli groups.

The State of Israel

29 November 1947. The United Nations voted to divide Palestine into two separate states – one Jewish, one Arab. The Jews accepted this, but the Palestinians totally rejected it. On 15 May 1948 the British (with a sigh of relief) finally withdrew their peacekeeping forces.

David Ben Gurion declared the State of Israel and immediately five Arab states (Egypt, Jordan, Iraq, Syria and Lebanon) invaded – their aim was to drive Israel into the sea. The result of this War of Independence was that Israel gained a lot of new territory, while Jerusalem was split in two. East Jerusalem (including the Wailing Wall and the Temple Mount) was in Jordanian hands. West Jerusalem was now part of Israel.

Up to Date

Three major conflicts have followed since then…

- **Six Day War** In 1967, Israeli troops took the Sinai Desert from Egypt, captured the Golan Heights in Galilee and the West Bank of the River Jordan. Paratroopers (sent in by bus!) stormed East Jerusalem and reunited the city under the government of Israel.

- **Yom Kippur War** In 1973, Egypt and Syria attacked Israel during one of its major religious festivals. There were major Israeli losses.

- **Invasion of Lebanon** Following a partial invasion in 1978, the Israeli army launched a full-scale attack on its northern neighbour in 1982. Their aim was to wipe out the forces of the PLO (Palestine Liberation Organisation) and to make safe Israel's northern border.

Israel now lives in a state of uneasy peace. Outside, there is hostility from the surrounding Arab nations and Israel regularly gets a bad press internationally. And from inside the Palestinians in the occupied territories (especially Gaza and the West Bank) are increasingly restless for a solution to their dispute with Israel over whose land it really is.

Israel's Youth Hostels

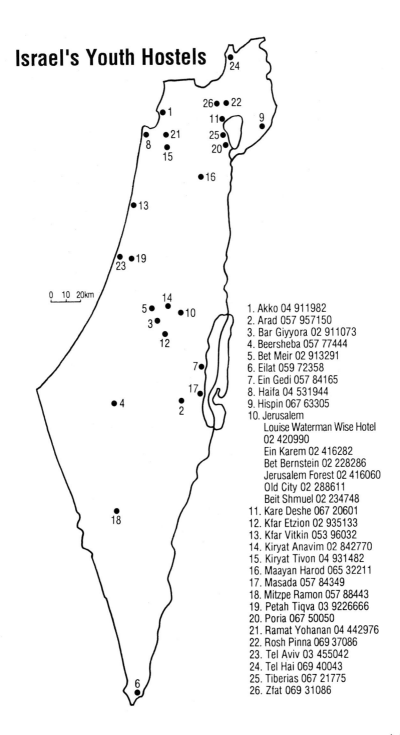

1. Akko 04 911982
2. Arad 057 957150
3. Bar Giyyora 02 911073
4. Beersheba 057 77444
5. Bet Meir 02 913291
6. Eilat 059 72358
7. Ein Gedi 057 84165
8. Haifa 04 531944
9. Hispin 067 63305
10. Jerusalem
    Louise Waterman Wise Hotel
    02 420990
    Ein Karem 02 416282
    Bet Bernstein 02 228286
    Jerusalem Forest 02 416060
    Old City 02 288611
    Beit Shmuel 02 234748
11. Kare Deshe 067 20601
12. Kfar Etzion 02 935133
13. Kfar Vitkin 053 96032
14. Kiryat Anavim 02 842770
15. Kiryat Tivon 04 931482
16. Maayan Harod 065 32211
17. Masada 057 84349
18. Mitzpe Ramon 057 88443
19. Petah Tiqva 03 9226666
20. Poria 067 50050
21. Ramat Yohanan 04 442976
22. Rosh Pinna 069 37086
23. Tel Aviv 03 455042
24. Tel Hai 069 40043
25. Tiberias 067 21775
26. Zfat 069 31086

INDEX

INDEX